The
Garland Library
of
War and Peace

The
Garland Library
of
War and Peace

Under the General Editorship of

Blanche Wiesen Cook, *John Jay College, C.U.N.Y.*

Sandi E. Cooper, *Richmond College, C.U.N.Y.*

Charles Chatfield, *Wittenberg University*

WAR
and its Alleged Benefits

by
Jacques Novicow
(Yakov Aleksandrovich Novikoff)

with an introduction by
Norman Angell

with a new introduction
for the Garland Edition by
Sandi E. Cooper

Garland Publishing, Inc., New York & London
1971

International Standard Book No. ISBN 0-8240-0274-1

Library of Congress No. LC 75-147482

Printed in the United States of America

Introduction

This short book was one of the few works of the Russian-born sociologist, Jacques Novicow (Yakov Aleksandrovich Novikoff) to be translated into English. During his lifetime, Novicow (1849-1912) was apparently as little known in the English-speaking world as he was in his native land, although French, Italian and German readers were familiar with his work. Except for his studies as a young man at the University of Odessa and for a brief foray into Russian politics in 1905, Novicow took little part in Russian life. His writings were mainly in French.[1] International peace was the consuming interest of his work and he explored its problems from the

---

[1]*Biographical information is scanty indeed. According to the entry under his name in* Novyi Entsiklopedicheskii Slovar *(Petrograd, 1916), XXVIII, 726, Novicow attended the zemstvo congresses in Moscow during 1905 as a delegate of the Kherson zemstvo. Generally, he lived the life of a scholar writing in western tongues and publishing abroad. Réné Worms, a Parisian sociologist, described Novicow in his obituary as a "utilitarian" thinker whose "writings are those of a man of action but also those of a convinced and generous idealist." See* Jacques Novicow" in Revue Internationale de Sociologie *XX (Paris, July, 1912) 481-483.*

Novicow characterized himself as a "free thinker" who had abandoned the orthodoxy of his parents, and had no attachment to any government. See footnote #3 to his article "Alsace-Lorraine" in Revue Internationale de Sociologie *XX (November, 1912) 757.*

Apparently he was financially independent and could travel and conduct his researches without having to work at any profession.

perspective of sociology. Novicow was a true intellectual in the rational, liberal tradition. He shared the positivist faith that the trained human mind could reason beyond the influence of daily prejudices and politics. Working as a sociologist during the early years of the history of that discipline, Novicow was as concerned with developing its methodology as he was with uncovering its "truths." [2] *A devotee of the western tradition, a compelling orator, an indefatigable scholar, he produced seventeen full length books on social, political, historical and economic topics as well as countless articles which appeared in a great variety of western journals. He helped organize and administer the Institut International de Sociologie (Paris) and found time to participate actively in the work of the Universal Peace Congresses. Charles Richet, professor of medicine at the Sorbonne and an active peace worker, wrote of Novicow after his death*

---

[2]*In the 1880's when Novicow's sociological works began to appear, he was clearly a proponent of the "organic" school of sociology which viewed societies as hierarchical systems wherein differing, unequal strata each served essential functions in the operation of the whole. Novicow was no egalitarian — he assigned to the social "élites" the most important functions.*

Frequently he employed metaphors comparing societies to healthy or diseased individuals or biological systems — or organisms. See particularly, Les Luttes entre les sociétés humaines et leurs phases successives *(originally published in Paris: Félix Alcan, 1893; republished in the Garland series);* Conscience et volonté sociales *(Paris: Félix Alcan, 1897) and "Essai de notation sociologique" in* Revue Internationale de Sociologie *III (Paris, 1895), 280. Finally, his work* La Théorie organique des sociétés: défense de l'organisme *(Paris: Giard et Brière, 1899) was the most explicit statement of the organic position in sociology which he held.*

INTRODUCTION

> He was an internationalist among internationalists. Speaking French, Italian, Greek and Russian with the same ease, he knew the literature of these various countries and he extended his thinking beyond the borders of his own country. He described himself, proudly and justly as a European. And he used his impartiality admirably to fight the prejudices of all Europeans.[3]

Besides his major concern, the problem of war and peace and the role of violence in history and society, Novicow developed interests in broad questions of social justice, including the improvement of the role and lot of women in modern society.[4] Socialism too attracted his interest, although he rejected its premises. In his work as a sociologist who analyzed the effects of the international anarchy upon societies, he was entirely sympathetic to the plight of the poor and the overburdened classes. But to the "social question" he refused to apply the cooperative formulae espoused by the socialists, since such would imply — in Novicow's assessment — an artifical rejection of the eternally valid and socially essential ingredient of healthy competition among men. Nonetheless, Novicow's rejection of socialism never

[3] *Charles Richet, preface to Novicow, L'Alsace-Lorraine: Obstacle à l'expansion allemande, (Paris: Félix Alcan, 1913). This book was published after Novicow's death.*

[4] *See L'Affranchissement de la Femme (Paris: Félix Alcan, 1903). Novicow also participated in a special meeting conducted by the Société de Sociologie de Paris, July, 1910 on the subject "Household Duties and Feminism," the transcript of which appears in the* Revue Internationale de Sociologie *(Paris: 1910), pp. 499 et seq.*

7

reached the heights of repugnance of the usual nineteenth century liberal critics, such as Gustave Molinari. Never did Novicow deny the existence of the social tensions which gave life to the expanding socialist movements nor did he deny the human rights of the socially disenfranchised to a better existence. But Novicow tied the improvement in the lot of the miserable to the curtailment of inefficient, useless and unproductive expenditures made on armaments. In the long run, he argued, the solution to the "social question" was intimately connected to the solution of the international anarchy. Both of these solutions could, but not necessarily would, be found through the extension of liberal principles.[5] While Novicow basically disagreed with socialist principles, he was friendly with a number of socialist leaders and a frank admirer of socialist organization which he recommended as a model to the international peace movement.

In addition to rejecting socialism, Novicow was impatient of extremist, vulgar social Darwinism. In many ways, the thrust of his writings parallelled those of Pyotr Kropotkin, author of Mutual Aid.[6] Novicow and Kropotkin criticized the abuse of the idea of struggle by numerous social Darwinists and the denial of the degree of cooperation among animal and

[5] Les Gaspillages des sociétés modernes: contribution à l'étude de la question sociale. (Paris: Félix Alcan, 1894).

[6] Reprinted as part of the Garland series from the 1902 edition.

human species. In one particularly biting passage, Novicow described social Darwinism as "the doctrine which considers collective homicide as the cause of progress among the human species."[7] At a calmer moment, he did recognize that there were variations and schools among the social Darwinists, ranging from "liberal" to "reactionary," but he was consistently repelled by the use of Darwin to justify the cruelest visions of human relations and to rationalize constant increases in military budgets.

Novicow's analysis of society and its problems asserted and affirmed a liberal view of reality which hoped for, but did not promise, improvement and progress. While he believed that social problems, including war, could be resolved or transformed by the application of enlightened reason, he never indicated that the process was inevitable. Novicow's work serves as a reminder that not all pre-1914 intellectual activity acted as the "precursor" of anxiety-ridden, irrationalist, sub-conscious or even "pre-fascist" modes of thought which exploded after World War I. Nor was his "liberalism" a rigid, mechanical and non-humane philosophy suitable to a stereotypic efficiency expert of materialism.

War and Its Alleged Benefits *was the work of Novicow in the guise of a publicist and journalist. Herein he undertook to write up a summary of his ideas for a popular audience to consume in rapid order. The book is a typical piece of anti-war polemic*

[7]La Critique du Darwinisme sociale *(Paris: Félix Alcan, 1910), p. 3.*

from the period before 1914. It was usually Novicow's style to take issue with articles and books that espoused the versions of social Darwinism which he rejected. In this short work, there are repeated criticisms of his bêtes noires — authors such as Max Jähns, G. Valbert, Gustave le Bon, Gumplowicz, Ratzenhofer and even Ernest Renan, all of whom are excoriated for justifying war and violence as essential ingredients of human nature and survival. Novicow's little book is an oversimplified version of much of his other work and thus, it is tempting to launch devastating criticism against it. He was obviously too superficial in the second chapter, "One-Sided Reasoning," which took to task those who upheld defensive war. Discussions of the virtues of defenders usually ignored the existence of aggressors. Yet, Novicow himself did not go on to develop the whole issue of aggression — at least not in this work. It remains as painful an omission on his part as it was on the part of those he criticized.

Again, in his chapter on "Physiological Effects," Novicow did not entirely repudiate the social Darwinist dichotomy between stronger and weaker races or peoples. The sympathetic reader yearns for some reassessment of the notion that a people or nation is intrinsically "weaker" because it has been defeated in battle. Nonetheless, the humanity and sheer common sense of the author emerges on every page. "No," he maintained, "our neighbor is not the sole aggressor. We, too, are aggressors." Militarism has advantages for a very small number of people; "the people hate war. There is not a man in ten thousand who would willingly . . . enter a campaign . . . it may be stated without fear of error that from the Ural Mountains to the Atlantic, the Europeans have the utmost horror of conscription and war."[8]

In the conclusion of his book, Novicow pleaded for recognition of the real enemies of mankind — not other human beings but rather the pestilences and miseries which stalked the earth. He estimated that roughly 5,000,000,000 work days were annually spent on the "displacement of boundary lines."[9] *Obviously all these hours and the wealth financing them could be used for a far better and more humane purpose.*

Sandi E. Cooper
Division of Social Sciences
Richmond College (C.U.N.Y.)

---

[8]War and Its Alleged Benefits, *pp. 109-111.*
[9]Ibid., *p. 150.*

11

W A R

AND ITS ALLEGED BENEFITS

WAR

AND ITS ALLEGED BENEFITS

BY

J. NOVIKOW

WITH AN INTRODUCTION BY

NORMAN ANGELL

Author of "The Great Illusion"

LONDON
WILLIAM HEINEMANN
1912

CONTENTS

PAGE

INTRODUCTION vii

CHAPTER I

WAR AN END IN ITSELF I

CHAPTER II

ONE-SIDED REASONING 8

CHAPTER III

WAR A SOLUTION 15

CHAPTER IV

PHYSIOLOGICAL EFFECTS 23

CHAPTER V

ECONOMIC EFFECTS 31

CHAPTER VI

POLITICAL EFFECTS 43

CONTENTS

CHAPTER VII

PAGE

INTELLECTUAL EFFECTS 55

CHAPTER VIII

MORAL EFFECTS 69

CHAPTER IX

SURVIVALS, ROUTINE IDEAS, AND SOPHISTRIES . 86

CHAPTER X

THE PSYCHOLOGY OF WAR 101

CHAPTER XI

WAR CONSIDERED AS THE SOLE FORM OF STRUGGLE 117

CHAPTER XII

THE THEORISTS OF BRUTE FORCE 129

CHAPTER XIII

ANTAGONISM AND SOLIDARITY 141

INTRODUCTION

IF the history of human progress reveals anything, it surely reveals this : that some of the best human emotion has been expended upon some of the worst possible objects. Not only do we find an incalculable amount of endeavour and suffering and self-sacrifice expended upon futile things—a life passed upon a bed of spikes, or at the top of a pillar, eaten by vermin— but we are continually confronted with facts such as that millions of men, through thousands of years, were persuaded that it was their bounden duty to enforce a given religious belief by any means whatsoever—force, cruelty, torture. It

INTRODUCTION

was from no defect of morality or good intention that humanity went astray on these matters so long : the more moral the man, the greater often was the futility of his life and the cruelty of his acts.

Now much good work in the cause of peace has, in the past, been nullified by overlooking the truth which lies at the bottom of the phenomenon just indicated. It has too often been assumed that what is needed in order to clear up the difficulties of international relationship is a better moral tone—greater kindliness, and so forth—oblivious of the fact that the emotion of humanity repelling from war may be more than counteracted by the equally strong moral emotions we connect with Patriotism : war *may* occasion suffering, says the patriot ; but men are, and should be, prepared to endure suffering for their country. That men are called upon to suffer for an ideal may be the very fact which constitutes its attraction to them. The Pacifist appeal to humanity has failed because the militarist believes that he too is working and suffering for humanity.

The difference between the Pacifist and the Militarist is not, at bottom, a moral one at all (assuming that we take the best statement of each case) but an intellectual one, and, if we are to bring about that Political Reformation in Europe which is to liberate us from the militarist burden, as the religious Reformation liberated Europe from religious oppression, the processes will have to be intellectual : just as men grew out of the absurdity of futile self-torture because the ideal it represented, when tested in the light of reason, was seen to be, even on moral grounds, unsound, so, in like manner, will men see when they apply their reason to the task— and not before—that the ideals represented by war are unsound alike on grounds of morality and self-interest (you cannot of

course, in reality, separate the two,
though our thought does continually
separate them).

There was as much good intention, as
much readiness and self-sacrifice in the
Europe of the fifth century as of the
twentieth; there is, perhaps, as much to-
day in Hindustani or Arabia as in
England; but what differentiates the
twentieth from the fifth century, or
Arabia from England, is a difference of
ideas, due to hard mental work: the
prime, if not the sole factor of progress is
hard thinking.

And nowhere do we need it more than
in the science of international politics.
The very foundations of that science have
been vitiated by the survival of a termin-
ology which is in reality the legacy of
Roman or Feudal conditions, but which
woefully distorts things when applied to
modern conditions. Absurdities which do
not stand the test of the very first analysis

are still persisting as unchallenged axioms, because the fundamental notions which underlay them have not been tested in the light of changed conditions.

At the head of the small band of men who, on the continent of Europe, have tackled this problem along the lines indicated here—as an intellectual problem to be stated in terms of national self-interest—stands Jacques Novikow. Like all best equipped for this task, he is a Sociologist first, and a Pacifist after. His work, much of which does not deal with the special problem of war at all, but with the larger sociological problems, is contained in a round score of books which constitute some of the most pregnant and suggestive contributions to serious European literature of the last ten years. And it is a somewhat humorous commentary on the fears which have been expressed, that this country is in danger of progressing more rapidly in Pacifism than its rivals, that

INTRODUCTION

Novikow's work, familiar to the best minds of the continent for so many years, has not yet appeared in English dress. Even this little book found its way to America before being presented to the English public.

Because Novikow is a Sociologist first, his work represents an objective study of the science of human relationship, of most of the forces which have, in the past, and are destined in the future, to shape that relationship. He has come to this task without sentimental, religious or political prepossessions of any sort. The reader will find here no sentimental declamation of the type that may perhaps have irritated him in some presentations of the case for peace. This is an essay in "Realpolitik," as distinct from what the Germans call "Sentimentalpolitik." "If it could be demonstrated," says Novikow, "that war made for the general advantage of mankind, I should be in favour of war." But his observation of all the complex phenomena of man's life on the planet has convinced him that only to the extent to which mankind gets away from what he has termed " L'Illusion Spoliatrice " will general advance be made.

The quotation of this last phrase may perhaps excuse a personal note, in so far as it affects the author of " The Great Illusion "—the point goes a little beyond the mere personal interest of the two authors concerned. To whatever extent the book just mentioned and some of Novikow's work may run parallel is not due to any literary contact—to the study of the work of each by the other—but to the fact that existing political phenomena have prompted independently in the minds of both authors, similar reflection and identical conclusions. And the fact is sufficiently suggestive, especially in view of the difference of treatment adopted.

Until some time after the appearance

INTRODUCTION

of the book which formed the basis of
" The Great Illusion," Novikow's work
was unknown territory to me (I have
explored it pretty thoroughly since).
And yet, at the very time that I was
elaborating the propositions outlined in
" Europe's Optical Illusion " in terms of
the actual present day problems of Europe
and their relation to such matters as the
growth of trade, the Stock Exchanges
and the Bank Rate, Novikow was elucidat-
ing the same general principle which
underlies those propositions, in terms of
the more abstract sociological problems
based upon biological laws associated with
Darwin's name.

Novikow's " Darwinisme Social " appeared practically simultaneously with
" Europe's Optical Illusion ": it was
impossible for the one author to have seen
the work of the other—and yet, not only
are the general conclusions of the two
works identical, but the operation of the

same laws is traced, one in terms of
biology, and the other in terms of
economics : the Russian working in
Odessa and the Englishman in Paris had
pitched upon, and elaborated, quite independently, a series of social and economic
phenomena, which to both threw a new
light, and pretty much the same kind of
light, upon the gravest problem of our
time. As one American critic of this
present book—which can be read in an
hour, but which contains more arguments
against war in the abstract than anything
of similar bulk I know—has said : " By
very different roads but by pretty much
the same method of travel, Jacques
Novikow and Norman Angell have arrived
at the same destination."

Though the destination be the same, the
roads lead through such very different
country that it is well worth the while of
any reader who has found any value
whatever in " The Great Illusion," or

INTRODUCTION

my two earlier works, to read every line
of Novikow's upon which he can lay his
hands. And those who hope to do their
part in the creation of a saner public
opinion in Europe—which is the only
means, not merely of settling the arma-
ment problem, but certain other social
and moral problems not at first sight
connected therewith—should make themselves familiar with every fact, argument
and illustration that this little book
contains.

NORMAN ANGELL.

CHAPTER I

WAR AN END IN ITSELF

A GERMAN author, Max Jähns, in a work ardently apologising for war,[1] says : " War regenerates corrupted peoples, it awakens dormant nations, it rouses self-forgetful, self-abandoned races from their mortal languor. In all times war has been an essential factor in civilisation. It has exercised a happy influence upon customs, arts and science." [2] Some French authors hold the same views. At bottom, G. Valbert agrees with Max Jähns, and the great Ernest Renan says somewhere : " Let us cling with love to our custom of

[1] *Ueber Krieg, Frieden und Kultur*, Berlin, 1893.
[2] G. Valbert in the *Revue des Deux Mondes*, April 1, 1894, p. 695.

fighting from time to time, because war is the necessary occasion and place for manifesting moral force." [1]

Another writer, Dr. Le Bon, says : "One of the chief conditions for the upliftment of an enfeebled nation is the organisation of a very strong military force. It must always hold up the threat of a disastrous war." [2]

According to these authors, war has beneficial results. If war should be suppressed, those benefits would likewise disappear. War, then, is an end in itself.

Now, here we have the great, fundamental error from which innumerable other fallacies logically proceed. War never has been an end, whether for animals or man. Since living beings have peopled our sphere, they have killed one another without cease, every hour, every minute, every

[1] Quoted by P. Lacombe, *De l'histoire considérée comme science*, Paris, Hachette, 1894, p. 83.

[2] *Les lois psychologiques de l'évolution des peuples*, Paris, F. Alcan, 1894, p. 160.

second. But massacre has always been a means, not an end. When a lion strangles a deer, he does so for the sake of food. When he is satiated, he sleeps stretched in the sun. A hunter shoots birds that make a good dish. He disdains others, even if they come within reach of his gun. To waste his cartridges on them is to lose time and money.

Since the remotest periods men went to war only with some particular object in view. The goal striven for by every human being is enjoyment. If the death of one of his kind can procure him that, he will sacrifice him without pity.[1] But if such is not the case, he will not take the trouble to kill him, since purposeless work is the worst suffering.

War is carried on from one of the following motives : to kill one's fellow-

---

[1] Thus, Napoleon I. caused two million Frenchmen to be massacred in order in a degree to satisfy his self-love.

men for the sake of using them as food;
to deprive them of their women; to
obtain booty from them;[1] to impose a
religion, certain ideas, or a type of culture
upon them.

If a territory does not supply enough
animal food, war is sometimes made to
take prisoners and eat them.

As for the rape of women, it is now a
very infrequent practice, and I need not
dwell upon it.

Wars undertaken to obtain chattels have
been, and still are, rather general. But
the practice of redemption proves that in
this case, as in all others, fighting is solely
a means. Often to keep from being
pillaged, certain nations consented to pay
a tribute. If the sum seemed sufficient
to the aggressors, they accepted it, well
content not to have to go to battle.

Cæsar invaded Gaul. His aim was to

---

[1] The German word for war, *Krieg*, is derived from
the word *kriegen*, which means to take, to carry off.

make himself master of that country for the sake of a number of advantages, which it would take too long to enumerate here. It was a severe war. But if the Gauls had submitted at once, Cæsar would not have taken the trouble to go on a single campaign or kill a single man.

In the sixteenth century the Flemings embraced Protestantism. Philip II. wanted to force them to become Catholics again. If at the first threat from the king of Spain the Flemings had returned to the religion of their ancestors, Philip would not have sent a single soldier to the Netherlands.

The Austrian Government centralised all the provinces of its empire. That offended the nationalism of the Magyars. If when Francis Joseph ascended the throne he had consented to grant their wishes, they would not have gone to war in 1848.

I have heard the following opinion expressed : " At this time retrogressive ideas are triumphing. If that continues, Europe is lost. A general war is needed to set us on a better path. The conquered nations will be obliged to mend their ways. Enlightened by defeat, they will reform their ancient institutions. The conquerors will of necessity do the same, and liberalism will carry the day." The person who so expressed himself was ready to see a million men sacrificed (a general war in Europe would result in that number of victims at the very least) for the triumph of his ideas. A rather cruel method of propaganda, it must be admitted, but here, as in every other case, carnage is a means, not an end.

Thus, the object of war has been in turn, cannibalism, spoliation, intolerance and despotism ; none of which have ever been held to be beneficial. Then, how the means by which those objects have been attained, that is, war, can be beneficial, is an incomprehensible mystery.

6

WAR AN END IN ITSELF

As we now see, all we need do is abandon nebulous metaphysics and take our stand for an instant on the ground of concrete realities to see all the alleged benefits of war vanish away like smoke.

War might be an end in itself, it might produce results favourable to mankind, but that only if suffering and death were enjoyable.   And everybody knows they are not.

CHAPTER II

ONE-SIDED REASONING

THOSE who attribute moral benefits to war are guilty of an astonishing fallacy. They think merely of defence, never of attack.

" It is necessary to overcome some repugnance," says Sismondi,[1] " to venture to say that war is necessary to humanity, that even those private battles called duels preserve some of our virtues. Neverthe-less, we have seen that when nations renowned of old for their valour have been freed from all danger, when they have been forbidden the use of arms, when they have lost that standard of

---

[1] *Histoires des républiques italiennes*, Paris, Furne, 1840, vol. ii, p. 172.

honour which makes them brave death—
we have seen them lose, along with their
military courage, the very strength that
keeps up the domestic virtues. We have
seen them debased in peace by the very
cause that exposed them to defeat. And
we have convinced ourselves that to be
worthy to live man must learn to brave
danger and death."

These words are typical. Without
doubt, to defend one's rights at peril of
death is a most generous deed ; without
doubt, the communities unwilling to
bring themselves to do so soon fall into
the lowest state of degradation ; only—
we forget the other side of the question.
That the A's should be obliged to defend
their rights with their lives, there must
perforce be B's who violate those rights
also at the risk of their lives. Defence
necessarily involves attack.

Another example : " Max Jähns finds
nothing to say against wars of expansion,

9

but the wars that he prefers to all others are those waged in self-defence. They are the noblest and most glorious."

Mr. Jähns's blindness is truly surprising. How is a defensive war possible without an offensive war ? The weakest house of cards will not fall unless it is blown upon. The timidest man in the world can live in tranquillity if nobody violates his rights ; in other words, if nobody attacks him.

Mr. Jähns's book contains another pearl of one-sided reasoning. He justifies war on the ground that it is a right. He says, "The first and most evident right of all is the right to live."[2] Assuredly. But it is not the right to kill. Now, without murderers, there never would be any murdered.

We see some races fallen into deep debasement; the Bengalis, for instance.

---

[1] *Revue des Deux Mondes, loc. cit.,* p. 693.
[2] *Revue des Deux Mondes, loc. cit.,* p. 699.

ONE-SIDED REASONING

Since time immemorial they have submitted to conquest without the faintest
protest. Whoever the invader that pos-
sessed himself of their country, they
obeyed him without offering resistance.
The degradation of the Bengalis is heart-
rending. They utterly lack virile energy.
They are fawners, liars, cheats; in a
word, the scum of humanity.

The Bengalis are said to have fallen so
low because they never knew how to
conduct war and defend their country.
Nobody reflects that the Bengalis fell so
low because other people attacked them
and made war upon them, though that is
the correct way of viewing the question.
Suppose Bengal had never been invaded
by a number of crowned brigands bearing
the pompous name of conquerors; suppose
the inhabitants of Bengal had never been
obliged by the knife at their throat to
give up nine-tenths of their revenues to
the aggressors; suppose their rights had

never been violated and they had not been tyrannised over in the most infamous fashion. They would have held their heads higher; they would have been proud and dignified, and perhaps might have taken for their motto, *Dieu et mon droit.* If nobody had oppressed the Bengalis, there would have been no need for them to resort to lying, cheating, fawning. Man acquires those vices because he thinks them profitable. In a country in which all rights are respected, nobody is tempted to commit base deeds, which are absolutely useless and always troublesome.

Why did the Bengalis become the scum of humanity? Because they were unable to defend themselves, say the short-sighted who think by rote. Not at all. It is because they were attacked. That is the first and foremost reason.

It is only by the fallacy of one-sided reasoning that moral benefits can be attributed to war.

ONE-SIDED REASONING

When within a civil community one man makes an attempt upon the rights of another, our sympathies go to the victim, our hatred and contempt to the aggressor. X tried to murder Y. Y is wounded. We take care of him, we show the greatest solicitude on his behalf. As for X, society places its ban upon him. He is a criminal. Every honourable man is ashamed to associate with him. He is condemned and put to death. But our morals take a sudden turn when international relations enter into the question. By the strangest aberration, all our sympathy and admiration go to the one that transgresses the rights of his fellow-creatures, to the glorious conqueror. Our hatred and contempt go to the victims. But for the succession of brigands that invaded Bengal, the people of that country would never have taken on their present vices. Strange—we scorn the unfortunate corrupt, but not the vicious corrupters.

13

WAR

In short, to risk one's life in defending one's rights, to prefer death to disgrace, is great, beautiful, generous.   But it is base and vile to violate the rights of others, to steal, pillage, despoil, and tyrannise over people's consciences.   Now, every aggressor of necessity commits those misdeeds.   Since there can be no war without an aggressor, war is one of the principal causes of the degradation of the human race.

CHAPTER III

SOME years ago the world's disarmament was being discussed. The king of Denmark expressed himself emphatically in favour of it. The *Moscow Gazette*,[1] commenting upon his opinion, said : " Is disarmament possible ? We think not. Too much gall has gathered among the European nations. . . . War is the one method of deciding international questions." At the western end of the continent in Paris, the *ville-lumière*, the very same view finds expression. " A secret instinct informs people," says Mr. Valbert, " that gross evils require gross

---

[1] March 30 or 31, 1894.

remedies, and great crises, violent solutions that the word does not always work miracles, that force has its rôle to play in human affairs, that in the long run certain evils become intolerable, that an end must be made of those evils at all costs, and that an end cannot be made of them except by war."[1]

It is difficult to decide what is more revolting in these sentiments, their cold cruelty or their illogicality.

The *Moscow Gazette* cites facts in support of its opinions. "From the year 1496 B.C. to 1861 A.D., in 3,358 years, there were 227 years of peace and 3,130 years of war, or thirteen years of war to every year of peace. Within the last three centuries there have been 286 wars in Europe." And Mr. Valbert says : "From the year 1500 B.C. to 1860 A.D. more than 8,000 treaties of peace meant to remain in force forever were concluded.

[1] *Revue des Deux Mondes, loc. cit.,* p. 696.

The average time they remained in force is two years." [1]

I put this categoric question to the advocates of war : "If war is able to decide differences, how is it that 8,000 wars have settled nothing, and that in this year of our Lord we feel the necessity for the eight thousand and first war? If more than 8,000 wars have settled nothing, what probability is there that the eight thousand and first, as if by magic, will suddenly decide all questions in dispute ? By what surprising change, by what incomprehensible miracle will that eight thousand and first war possess such extraordinary virtues ? " I should really like an explanation. It is worth the while to try and get one.

The illogicality of these backward thinkers is as prodigious in each particular case as in the general question. In France one constantly hears : " War is the only

[2] *Ibid.*, p. 692.

solution of the Alsace-Lorraine question."
If that is so, why did not the war of 1870
solve it ?   Now, if the war of 1870 did
not solve the Alsace-Lorraine question,
then war cannot solve that or any other
question. Indeed, let the Germans be
completely defeated and the situation will
remain the same as in 1871. The
Germans would then have lost a province
which in their opinion was " flesh of their
flesh and bone of their bone." They
would forge new weapons and await a
favourable opportunity for recapturing
Alsace-Lorraine, as they have done since
1648.   Where would the solution be ?

In 1871 the Germans thought they had
settled their differences with their neighbours on the west. By levying the indemnity of five milliards of francs they
thought they had drained France of her
last drop of blood. Napoleon I. also
thought he had *done* with Prussia after the
battle of Jena, when he took half its

territory and reduced its army to 40,000 men. Vain illusions of routine thinking, chimeras of human blindness! We might as well make up our minds that it will be just as ineffectual in the future as it has been in the past, to "drain a country of its last drop."

Speaking of the factions in the Italian cities in the middle ages, Massimo d'Azeglio says : " Each time a party came into power, it foolishly thought it could keep its position by unjust and violent methods. As a matter of fact, injustice and violence were the very causes that prevented any party from remaining in power for a length of time." [1]

The same is true of international questions. They will never be decided so long as violence is resorted to ; that is to say, so long as wars are carried on. The past is a guarantee of the future. If 8,000 wars have produced no result,

[1] *Niccolo de' Lapi*, Florence, le Monnier, 1866, p. 63.

one must be utterly devoid of reason to think that battles are a means of deciding international differences.

A question is decided only if it is adjusted in a way that the contending parties consider equitable. For example, when the English took Canada, they wanted to impose their language upon the French there. They used the most brutal means.[1] The armed revolt, in other words, the war, ended in a final outburst in 1857. It was followed by the military repression of the gallows. But soon England abandoned that absurd, superannuated policy. It gave up its efforts to denationalise the Canadians, realising that they had the right to be French, and it established in America an order of things just and equitable to all.

[1] One of the most horrible chapters in the history of England is the expulsion of the unhappy French Acadiens, which has remained in the memory of the people as the *grand dérangement.*

WAR A SOLUTION

Thus, at the banquet of the *Alliance Française* held on April 16, 1891, Mercier, governor of the province of Quebec, could say with truth: " Now our liberties are assured by a wise, generous constitution, under the enlightened direction of the statesmen of England. Our struggles are over."[1] Respect for others' rights, justice, mutual concessions, these are the means of settling disputes. Bloodshed never will succeed. Since the beginning of history wholesale murder has been committed thousands and thousands of times without solving anything. It will be committed thousands and thousands of times again without yielding a better result. Each war merely sows the seed of a future war.

One thing about wars deceives us. After frightful carnage, the belligerents are sometimes exhausted. They long for

[1] *Bulletin de l'Alliance Française*, April-June, 1891, p. 43.

tranquillity, and they appoint pleni-
potentiaries to settle their differences.
Since each side desires a cessation of
hostilities, each makes mutual concessions.
An adjustment is reached and a *modus
vivendi* is found equally acceptable to all
the parties involved. It is this good will,
this feeling for justice that leads to
solutions, it is not the hecatombs, it is
not the war preceding. If the same
spirit of concord had been displayed
beforehand, an agreement would un-
doubtedly have been reached. But since
the establishment of a more or less
equitable order of things assuring justice
and peace too often follows the bloodiest
wars, the mind is misled by a false
association of ideas. The regulation of
international differences is attributed to
the war, whereas, on the contrary, it is
due solely to respect for the rights of
others, to the spirit of equity, to good
will, and mutual concessions.

CHAPTER IV

ONE of the principal benefits attributed to war is that it operates for a selection favourable to the species. War, it is alleged, eliminates the degenerate races, assures the empire of the earth to vigorous, well-endowed races, and so constantly improves mankind.

There are few more egregious errors. It is easy to show that the selection resulting from war has *always* been the very reverse. It has invariably eliminated individuals physiologically the most perfect, and has allowed the weakest to survive. War has not hastened mankind's improvement, but retarded it. Improvement has taken place not as a result of, but in spite of, war.

Since the most ancient times men of the soundest constitutions, the most vigorous men, have gone off to fight. The weak, the sick, the deformed have remained at home. So, every battle carried away some of the select, leaving behind the socially unproductive. Besides, in the army itself there are brave men and cowards. The brave are certainly the more perfect physiologically. Since they go to the front, more of them fall. Thus a second selection is added to the first to contribute to the elimination of the physically superior.

It is said that in savage times war was carried on between the tribes without pity. The victors killed off the defeated to the very last man, and married the women. In that way a cross-breeding favourable to the race took place. That would be true but for one condition, if there had been no killed among the victors; which, we know from history, never was the case. Certain encounters were so desperate that the number of killed on each side was equal; sometimes, in fact, greater on the side of those that remained masters of the field. Hence the number of handsome men who could win women was less after a battle than before. War, therefore, has always produced a selection for the worse instead of for the better.

Besides, to kill all the defeated was impossible. A number saved themselves by flight. And soon the victors, instead of killing the vanquished people, reduced them to slavery. The slaves married and brought forth children. War, after eliminating the braver, permitted the weaker to live. It did not bring about a favourable selection.

In our days the conquerors do not marry the wives of the conquered. On the contrary, the hatred excited by conflicts prevents marriage between the belligerents. The number of marriages between the Frenchmen and Germans is certainly less since 1870 than before. Thus, the alleged benefit attributed to war in the period of savagery is entirely absent in the period of civilisation.

" The stronger, the healthier, the more normally constituted a young man is," says Ernst Haeckel,[1] " the more likely he is to be killed by rifles, cannons, and similar engines of civilisation." The recruiting officers are pitiless. If a young man has the least physical defect, even so slight a thing as bad teeth or poor sight, they reject him. The very flower of each generation are chosen for the butcheries. Wherein lies the favourable selection here? One must be quite prejudiced to maintain that war nowadays improves the race.

Napoleon caused the killing of

[1] *Natürliche Schöpfungsgeschichte*, 4th ed., Berlin, 1873, p. 154.

3,700,000 men. Who dares assert that those men had the poorest constitutions? Everybody knows they were the pick of Europe. After the Paraguayan war " the virile population disappeared almost completely. None remained but the sick and the disabled." [1] Would it be right to say that such a condition improved the Paraguayan race?

One more point. In man the procreative passion reaches its culmination during the very years he spends in the barracks. Surely no one would say that the soldier in the army has the same opportunity for bringing forth children as the citizen at home. As a result, at the very time when the select in generation desire the most strongly to insure progeny, they are prevented from doing so. Those whom the recruiting officers reject, on the contrary, have every oppor-

[1] E. Reclus, *Nouvelle géographie universelle*, vol. xix, p. 503.

tunity to propagate their kind. Their offspring become more and more numerous, and through militarism the races tend to degenerate not only in times of war, but even in times of absolute peace.

Other factors counteract and, in a large degree, weaken the disastrous effects of war. That is why we do not see the process of degeneration in its general outline.

If wars perfect the races, then the most belligerent nations should be the handsomest. But such is not the case. In fact, the contrary is true. The English are most certainly one of the handsomest people on earth. They are also the least warlike, since they alone, of all the European nations, have abolished compulsory military service.

It cannot be denied that athletic exercise, sports of all kinds, contribute to the improvement of the animal man. They give strength to the muscles and suppleness to the body, and develop energy and endurance. In short, they tend to perfect the individual physiologically. Now, in our days, a strange phenomenon may be observed. The practice of athletics may be said to be in inverse ratio to militarism. In England sports are carried on on an immense scale—the boat races between the Oxford and Cambridge crews are a national event—less so in the western countries of the European continent, and almost not at all in Russia. When physical exercise has been imposed upon a young man by the brutal officer-teachers of our modern armies, it inspires a disgust which clings to him the rest of his life.

So we see that from a physiological point of view war has never contributed to the improvement of the human race. It has always had the opposite tendency. If, nevertheless, improvement has taken place, it was produced, not thanks to, but in spite of, war. The principal factors of improvement are love and death.

The handsomest men and women are most likely to excite sexual passion, the ugly and deformed less so. From this proceeds a favourable selection. In addition, the incapable are thrown back into the lower classes of society. Upon them are imposed the hardest, the most dangerous, and the least remunerative work. Since they have less comfort, mortality among them is greater than among those who are better off. These two factors constantly operate to eliminate the physically inferior. The limited extent of the present book prevents me from enlarging upon this point. I will write of it in detail in a special work.

CHAPTER V

ECONOMIC EFFECTS

THE greater number of wars have arisen from a desire to appropriate the wealth of others. Expeditions were conducted for obtaining chattels, then for obtaining land, finally for obtaining the proceeds from taxes levied upon entire nations. The idea that we can enrich ourselves more speedily by seizing the possessions of our neighbours than by working ourselves is one of the notions most deeply embedded in the human mind. It is so persistent that in our own days it is accepted even by highly distinguished economists. "Since men are unequal in strength," says Mr. de

WAR

Molinari,[1] "the stronger can seize upon the product of the weaker men's work with less expenditure of labour and energy than they would have to employ if they themselves were to produce." This has never been so, or, rather, it has been so in appearance, but not in reality. War has always cost more effort than has direct production. Besides, the trouble connected with it easily vies with the nuisance of working. The profession of a soldier involving danger, suffering, and fatigue, clearly, is one of the hardest professions. So, since ancient times, it has been held in horror by all men. As soon as a man could get out of performing military service he did so. Often nowadays people mutilate themselves in order not to have to become soldiers. Do we ever see a man cut off a finger that he should not have to be a locksmith, or a mason, or an engineer, or a painter?

[1] *Science et religion*, Paris, Guillaumin, 1894, p. 17.

Those trades and nearly all others, we may then infer, are considered pleasanter than the soldiering profession.

But the annoyances produced by war do not stop with the cessation of hostilities. The day after the victory is harder, perhaps, than the day of battle. Of old, one of the greatest advantages attached to conquest seemed to be the possibility of making slaves. Then, thanks to the labour of the vanquished, the master could live in idleness and pomp. What, ostensibly, could be pleasanter? But the reality was entirely different. In the first place, slave labour is less productive than free labour. Experience a thousand times repeated has proved that countries into which slavery has been introduced do not prosper so well as countries employing free labour. Our enjoyment comes in the largest measure from public wealth, that is, from the general wealth of the country. Therefore, if the general

D

wealth increases less quickly, we suffer personal damage. But more than that. A slave-master can do nothing all day, and his life is none the pleasanter on that account. The harder the work he imposes, the more hate and resentment he inspires. Oppression provokes private revenge and general revolts. From Pliny's letters we know that the great Roman lords, even those who treated their slaves humanely, lived in perpetual terror of their lives. At any moment, they feared they might be assassinated. The same condition prevailed in Russia in slave times. Often when proprietors went on an excursion in the country, they had to take an escort along to guard them against their peasants. Such an existence, it must be admitted, can have little delight. The feudal lords of the middle ages were no more fortunate. They lived in constant warfare and despoiled their neighbours with the most charming unrestraint. But, alas ! their lives were none the gayer for that. They were compelled to shut themselves up in strong castles, which to us seem veritable dungeons. When they sallied forth they had to be accompanied by an armed guard. They were exposed to the constant threat of assault and death. In my opinion, I confess, there must have been slight enjoyment in an existence of that sort. Nowadays a man would deem himself profoundly miserable to live in the same circumstances. Think of what a nightmare it must have been not to be able to cross the threshold of one's home without seeing death lift its head and stalk before.

Wealth is nothing but a means, enjoyment the end. But, as we see, even if by war we can get possession of the wealth of others " with the least expenditure of labour and energy," we thereby obtain only a moderate amount of enjoyment.

WAR

But the very assumption that by war we wrest wealth with the least expenditure of effort will not stand criticism.

Every enterprise presupposes an outlay; in other words, capital. Capital represents accumulated work. If £4,000 are invested in a factory, it means that previously men worked a sufficient number of hours to earn that amount of money, which they saved and employed in the new undertaking. If the capital needed for the factory is £2,000, instead of £4,000, the smaller sum represents the work of half the number of hours.

Now, it is easy to prove that the capital used in military enterprises always has been greater than the capital for other enterprises. The more firmly men believed that war could enrich with " the least expenditure of labour and energy," the more they were drawn to practise that industry, consequently, to organise it thoroughly, to provide it with the most perfect equipment, in brief, to sink a larger and larger capital in it. That is what actually happened. In 1869 Laroque estimated at 19,500,000,000 francs, that is, £780,000,000, the value of the property, real and personal, appropriated to war in Europe alone.[1] It is without doubt no exaggeration to assume that that sum has been tripled at the very least since 1871. But let us be content to admit that it has merely been doubled; in which case the amount would be £1,600,000,000. But that is nothing. At present the maintenance of European armies costs £212,600,000 a year.[2] The money must come from somewhere. It is produced in the last analysis by the help of capital. So it is right to regard it as interest. Capitalising it, we obtain a principal approximating

[1] *La guerre et les armées permanentes*, Paris, C. Lévy, 1870, p. 246.
[2] See the *Riforma sociale*, April, 1894, p. 251.

£4,240,000,000. Thus, the aggregate of capitals used in military enterprises amounts to £5,840,000,000. There is only one other undertaking in the world that has required a larger sum, the railways. War, therefore, cannot enrich " with the least expenditure of labour and energy," since the capital employed in war is greater than that employed in nearly all other undertakings.

This has always been so. Military equipment diminished with the increase of security. Toulouse no longer needs to defend itself against Paris. So it is useless for Toulouse to fortify itself against Paris, or Paris against Toulouse. But of old, military equipment was indispensable. Assuredly, when Italy was divided up among a few dozen independent State engaged in constant warfare with one another, the capital used for military equipment must have been greater in proportion to the general wealth than it is to-day. If to-morrow Europe were to unite in a federation, the capital appropriated for war would be reduced in an enormous degree.

Thus, not only has war never enriched "with the least expenditure of labour and energy," but it has even decreased man's welfare. Wealth does not proceed from the possession of precious metals or any other commodity, but from the degree of the earth's adaptation to mankind's needs. Since 1648 war has cost the European nations alone £16,000,000,000.[1] It would not be exaggerating to say that in the entire historic period war has cost at least ten times that amount. Then, at the very lowest estimate, war has cost in all £160,000,000,000. What does that mean ? It means that a certain number of days of work, the money value of which is equal to that sum, were employed by men in killing one another. Suppose the same

[1] See my *Gaspillages des sociétés modernes*, p. 165.

effort had been expended in cultivating the soil, irrigating the fields, weaving cloth, building houses, levelling roads, channeling harbours, and so on, is it not perfectly clear that the world's face would be entirely different to-day ? We should be at least ten times as properous, or, in other words, the sum of suffering would have been perceptibly less for us unhappy beings.

Fortunately, one great point has already been won. Nobody nowadays asserts that war is lucrative. Formerly the opinion that war brought material benefits to the victors was universally accepted. But for two centuries the economists have been fighting with indomitable energy to prove that this notion is erroneous. They have won their cause. Even Mr. de Molinari's assertion, quoted at the beginning of this chapter, has reference to the past and not to the present. The Belgian economist labours under a delusion : war never has been lucrative, no more in the age of bronze than in this year of our Lord. However, though he makes this mistake in regard to the past, no one has demonstrated more clearly how ruinous war is in the present, despite the most brilliant victories. No one denies this truth, not even Mr. Valbert, who takes pleasure in enumerating the disasters produced by the military spirit. It is just because partisans of war have been beaten in this field that they seek another. They fall back on morality. I should really like to know what there is in common between fierce, pitiless butchery and morality. Yet, it appears, there is something in common. Mr. Valbert says so with truly praiseworthy assurance. " The moralist is ready to grant all that [economic losses], yet, no matter how great his respect for figures, he reserves his judgment. The question seems to him complex. Has it been proved that certain plagues have not had beneficial results ?   If it depended upon the moralist to suppress war, he might hesitate, perhaps."[1]   He might hesitate, perhaps ! There you have it, black on white !

[1] *Ibid.*, p. 695.

CHAPTER VI

ONE of the benefits attributed to war is that it founded those great nations, England, France, and Germany, which are such shining centres of civilisation.

In the middle ages it was said that God ruled the world through the intermediation of the Franks, *Gesta Dei per Francos*. Nowadays we believe that without the powerful States of modern Europe science, the arts, and literature would never have undergone their magnificent development. Suppose war in the past had been suppressed, what would the world be? Nothing but a dust-pile of little States, without cohesion, or force, or elasticity,

43

or consistency of ideas. Such a formless
chaos would mean primitive savagery in
all its hideousness and degradation.

Here we have a fallacy more monstrous
than any of the others. It is so foolish
and presupposes so complete an absence of
logic that one is positively stupefied to see
it maintained for more than a day.

In the first place, what does national
unity mean—the national unity of France,
for example ? It means that 38,000,000
men inhabiting 536,000 square kilometres
have found a way of adjusting their differences other than the beastly murder of one
another on fields of battle. Nowadays
Paris, Lyons, Marseilles, Bordeaux, Lille,
and Toulouse no longer wage war one
against the other. If they were to do so
to-morrow, France's unity would instantly
cease. Until 1861 Virginia, Kentucky,
Ohio, and Massachusetts lived in peace.
When the Southerners raised the standard
of revolt and began hostilities, the

American Union was ruptured. It was re-established and continued because the differences of the forty-six States, extending from the Atlantic to the Pacific, are adjusted by the Supreme Court at Washington, and not by carnage on battlefields.

National unity, therefore, is established on the day on which war ends.

Very well, you say, unity once established implies a state of peace, but was not war the instrument of its establishment? Never! War has always prevented unity, has thwarted and retarded it.

In the fourteenth century there were five to six hundred independent States in Germany, which constantly made war upon one another, and Germany's unity disappeared altogether. To restore it, it was necessary by force of arms to compel all the petty potentates to submit to a legal order, that is, to live in peace. This benefit is attributed to war. But no attention is paid to the fact that it is

precisely because those petty potentates
wanted to retain the right to wage war
that Germany's unity was unattainable for
so long a time. If after the tenth century
the different fractions of the German race
had not offered resistance to the establishment in common of really efficacious
institutions, Germany's unity might have
begun under Henry the Fowler and might
have lasted to the present. Hence, it was not
war that produced Germany's unity. War
prevented it for nearly nine centuries.

That is true of all other communities.
" No country," says Mr. Lacombe,[1] " had
so little militarism in the middle ages as
England." Consequently it was the first
to unify, while Germany's unity was the
slowest of all in forming, because even as
late as 1860 the kings of Hanover, Bavaria,
and Saxony wished to be free to declare
war on their neighbours when it seemed
good to them to do so There is another

[1] *L'histoire considérée comme science*, p. 349.

side to the question. The French of northern France took forcible possession of the land of the nation speaking the langue d'oc. Finally they assimilated them. The various southern dialects degenerated into the people's patois, and the langue d'oïl became the modern French, and was raised to the dignity of a literary language. French unity, then, was composed of two elements. It is thought it would never have been formed without the crushing of the southern element, and for that reason the existence of French unity is attributed to war.

To do justice to this point we must make a slight digression. Let us suppose that the Languedocian nationality had survived. Where would be the harm forsooth ? European civilisation, the source of our chief enjoyments, does not proceed from the fact that English is now spoken by 110,000,000 men, Russian by 80,000,000 German by 60,000,000, and

French by 45,000,000. The proportion
might have been different without alter-
ing the brilliancy of European civilisation for the better or the worse.
Civilisation is not made by the relative
number of spoken languages, but by
the sum of the scientific knowledge
and artistic treasures accumulated by
mankind. Europe is now divided into
eighteen main principalities. It might
have been divided into fifteen or
twenty-five, and civilisation would in
no wise have been affected. If, then,
instead of five great Latin nations we
should have had six with the addition of
the Languedocian, our wealth, our prosperity, and our intellectual development
would not have suffered the least setback.

But the French are still deluded by
the belief that linguistic boundaries of
necessity follow political boundaries.
The Hapsburg dynasty founded the
Austrian Empire at the beginning of the

sixteenth century by the acquisition of
Hungary and Bohemia. Nevertheless,
in neither Hungary nor Bohemia is
German spoken as French is spoken
in Provence. National assimilation is
governed by special factors. It is an
intellectual phenomenon that has its
special laws. This, however, is not the
place to enter into an examination of
them.[1] Suffice it to say that a language
and a culture may be propagated without the conquest of territories. Martin
Canal, in 1275, wrote a history of
Venice in French, because, he said, that
language " *est mult delectable à lire et à oïr* "
(is very pleasant to read and to hear).
But a little more, and the whole of
northern Italy would have done the same
as Canal. Dante's genius, Petrarch's, and
Boccaccio's assured pre-eminence to the
Italian language. Tuscany never widened

[1] I refer the reader to my *Politiques internationales*
and my *Luttes cntre sociétés humaines.*

its boundaries beyond the conventional limits, yet its language has become the literary language of the Apennine peninsula. Likewise Saxony never conquered Germany, yet its dialect became the literary language of that great country. On the other hand, the Turks ever since the fourteenth century have imposed their dominion on the Balkan peninsula without succeeding in imposing their language upon the Servians or Bulgarians. So nothing shows that even if southern France had not been conquered, French would not have been spoken to-day at Toulouse and Marseilles, just as it is at Brussels and Geneva, cities which have not formed a part of the kingdom of the Capets.

Brute conquest does not always result in linguistic expansion, and even from this point of view war is useless. It is not to wholesale slaughter on fields of battle that we owe the existence of those glorious historic entities called England, Germany, France, and Italy. It is to a galaxy of geniuses and talents of all kinds, to Dante, to Shakespeare, to Descartes, to Goethe, and the rest.

Thus, not only has war not formed the great national unities, but, on the contrary, it has even retarded their political organisation by several centuries.

I call the attention of the conventional advocates of brute force to another fact of infinitely greater importance. Suppress war and the unity of the human race in its entirety is instantly realised. Universal unity does not exist now because Germany, France, Russia, and the other States wish to remain free to declare war whenever it seems good to them to do so, like Saxony, Bavaria, and Hanover within the German nation, who not so long ago wished the same thing for themselves. Let the sovereign States renounce that liberty, let them find a way of adjusting their differences other than massacre—in brief, let them suppress war—and the unity of mankind is accomplished.

War, we see, for long centuries has prevented the formation of the great national unities. For more centuries to come it will prevent the unity of all mankind. Consequently, from a political point of view, as well as from all others, it produces evil and does not produce good.

In the preceding chapter we found that wars must in all have cost £160,000,000,000 at the very least. That probably represents approximately 4,000,000,000,000 days of work. All that prodigious effort went to give our continent the political boundaries now existing : that is, twenty-four independent States, a France of 536,000 square kilometres, a Germany of 540,000 square kilometres, a Servia of 48,000 square kilometres, etc. Now, all that effort has been as completely lost as if it had

CHAPTER VII

INTELLECTUAL EFFECTS

" If the philanthropists were to succeed
in suppressing war, they would, with the
best intentions in the world, be rendering
but a poor service to mankind. They
would by no means be working for the
ennoblement of our race. Unending
peace would plunge the nations into
dangerous lethargy." Thus Mr. Valbert.[1]
Melchior de Vogüé says : " The certainty
of peace (I do not say an actual state of
peace) would, before the expiration of
half a century, engender a state of corruption and decadence more destructive
of men than the worst wars." This

[1] *Ibid.*, p. 692.

quotation is taken from an article in the *Almanach Hachette* of 1894, entitled "Our Future." The appearance of this article is a very remarkable phenomenon. In their preface the editors say they wished the *Almanach* to be of service to everybody and to be so useful as to become indispensable. They wanted it to have the character of a small, popular encyclopedia. So a great many copies were published. Evidently the editors quoted De Vogüé because they considered the opinion he expressed to be one of the truths that cannot be disseminated too widely among the people. From the mere fact of its publication in the *Almanach* it acquires great importance for us.

It will not do to rest satisfied with words. Let us examine facts, and see if they confirm the opinion that war favours the development of human intelligence and prevents mental lethargy.

Men have always tried to improve

their condition. They have pursued agriculture in order not to suffer hunger, they have built houses to protect them against cold. Briefly, they have constantly tried to adapt their environment to their needs. When certain individuals have been freed from concern for their daily bread, they have turned to the arts, or literature, or science, or philosophy. A natural inclination leads from economic production to intellectual production, that is, to civilisation. This evolution presupposes a sufficient degree of security. For if man had been perpetually despoiled by his neighbour, wealth could not have accumulated, and intellectual needs could not have arisen. Thanks to certain fortuitous circumstances, it has come about that some countries have enjoyed sufficient security for a sufficient length of time for civilisation to progress and, in some places, to become brilliant. But all the nations did not advance at an equal

pace. While some made great progress
in technical knowledge, in literature,
science, and the arts, others lived in
savagery or barbarism. The latter,
consumed with envy at the sight of
the enjoyments of the civilised peoples,
often attacked and slaughtered them
without mercy. This happened time and
again in both hemispheres. In America,
in regions now occupied by entirely
savage Indians, we find the remains of
monuments showing that of old a
civilised people had lived in the country.

If there had been no war, it is clear,
such events would never have come to
pass. How can the periodic massacre of
more educated and cultivated people by
the more savage and ignorant people favour
the development of the human mind? I
for my part do not see how it possibly
can. Why should there have been more
light in Europe after a stupid Roman
soldier murdered Archimedes than there

had been before? I should like the partisans of slaughter to answer that question. As a matter of fact, human civilisation grew, not because of, but in spite of, war.

Reduce war to its simplest expression. X and Y have a dispute. X does not succeed in convincing Y. X gets angry, attacks Y, and kills him. Recourse to murder is perforce a reaction of the brute against the mind. This is true, and will continue to be true, of all wars. Barbarians see the life of a civilised people. They desire the same advantages. The intellectual procedure would be for them to produce wealth and educate themselves. The brutal procedure consists in practising spoliation by violence, that is, in practising war. On the instant that war breaks out, instead of two groups working to acquire a superior civilisation, only one pursuing that end remains. Therefore, beginning with the moment that hostilities commence, the sum of intelligence in humanity decreases.

War has always produced selection for the worse, not for the better. Its tendency has been to destroy communities more especially devoted to mental pursuits. Like the north wind, it has blown away some of the most delicate and sweetest-smelling flowers of mankind, Athens and Florence. Those marvellous centres perished from the blows of a base, brutal soldiery. Here we have an instance of how war furthers the development of the intelligence!

"It would seem," says Mr. E. Perrier,[1] "that after Aristotle, science, which he had set upon the right path, had nothing to do but to continue along that path. We should expect to see a marvellous scientific efflorescence follow upon the appearance of that great man. Unfortunately, the political divisions, the

[1] *Philosophie zoologique*, Paris, Alcan, 1884, p. 17.

60

wars, the invasions would not allow the continuation of the work begun in the East." The same is true of all times. The wars of the Revolution and the Empire caused a period of considerable arrestment to the intellectual development of Europe. The impulse given by the encyclopædists was weakened. Peace was needed before any advance could be made again.

If war favoured the activity of the mind, the most warlike people would be endowed with the most advanced scientific spirit. History demonstrates that the very reverse is true. War produces a selection for the worse. It has never favoured the intellectual development of humanity. No more has it prevented mental lethargy. On the contrary, it has always increased it.

In the sixteenth century the Flemings embraced Protestantism. The Spaniards thought that abominable. Suppose they

had sent forth a multitude of preachers to
Belgium to bring back the stray sheep.
What activity, what an intellectual ebulli-
tion would have taken place there! The
Spaniards would have preached in the
churches, they would have held lectures,
debates, great mass-meetings. They would
have published numerous writings. The
Flemings would have done the same.
Discussion would have sharpened their
wits. And the Spaniards either would
have been able to convince the Flemings
of the falseness of Protestantism, or they
themselves would have gone over to the
new ideas. Both events would doubtless
have arisen, and theological discussions
would have kept the people in a lively
mental state for many years. The study
of one science brings in its train the knowledge of others. To find arguments for
or against Catholicism one must have
made profound historic and philosophic
investigations. Briefly, a great intellectual

blossoming would have taken place in the Netherlands, and the country would have become the arena of immense intellectual activity.

But Philip II. did not for a single instant think of using persuasion. In a dispute in regard to something intellectual he did not wish to employ intellectual methods. He sent out troops, and carried on a war. Thanks to the defection of the Walloon nobility, the old Spanish troops beat the Flemings in the open country. Then the Duke of Alba came. He massacred, hung, tortured, and exiled thousands of persons. Terror hovered over those wretched provinces. The whole country sank into a state of dismal mental lethargy. The generous Flemish folk fell into so heavy a sleep that they have scarcely succeeded in rousing themselves even to this day. From this we can see how war prevents people from succumbing to "dangerous lethargy."

WAR

The apologists of slaughter should be
satisfied with that proof. We know, alas!
that what took place in the Netherlands
in the sixteenth century has been repeated
on a thousand other occasions.

In our day war is still one of the most
powerful causes of mental stagnation.

As a matter of fact, the more costly
war becomes, the more necessary large
political unities are to bear the expense.
In our days a State with fewer than
30,000,000 to 40,000,000 inhabitants
survives only by the tolerance and rivalry
of its more powerful neighbours. A
country cannot have a truly independent
policy unless it has a yearly budget of
£80,000,000. Now, many taxpayers are
needed for such a huge sum to be raised
annually. So we are forced to draw
together into large States of at least
500,000 square kilometres. What happens
then? A vast capital attracts all the
living forces of a nation. It becomes a

disproportionate, monstrous head. The rest of the country is drained of its blood. The provinces! The very word evokes in France the idea of unbearable boredom, of a torpidity resembling vegetable existence. Lately a French scholar complained of not being able to live in even the largest provincial cities. They offered him none of the resources indispensable to the study of his speciality. The same is the case in many other countries. Now, it is to war that we owe that adorable lethargy. Without war the leviathan States would have been useless. As long as Italy and Germany were divided into petty sovereignties, they were the sport of their powerful neighbours, France, Austria, Russia. Italy and Germany had to swim with the current; they unified themselves. Without war federations of little States would have been formed, in which a wise and harmonious balance would have been established between the institutions maintained in common and the local autonomy. But war intervened to disturb all that. Two things happened : either the petty potentates refused to give up the right to declare hostilities—in which case national unification was not achieved—or the danger from the outside and the royal power were the incentives to the establishment of a centralised government, which wiped out all traces of life in the minor centres. Lethargy was in direct ratio to international insecurity.

Moreover, when the army becomes a nation's chief organ, it naturally absorbs the most of its best nutritive substance. Compare the army budget with the public education budget. In France the proportion is 890,000,000 to 227,000,000 francs ; in Russia, 736,000,000 to 58,000,000. At present armed peace costs the Europeans £400,000,000 a year. Free the Europeans from that burden and they will doubtless devote a very much greater sum to their intellectual development.

Ceaseless warfare must certainly engender hatred between the combatants. Since the alien was always the one who harmed us, he was always treated with hostility. He was refused legal protection and civil privileges. That state of things in a great degree prevented men from living outside their fatherlands. War, therefore, set up the most difficult obstacles to a mixture of populations. Now, as we know, the crossing of races is a most powerful agent for their improvement, and the spread of ideas is a chief preventive of intellectual stagnation. Since war in a large measure hindered migrations, it has contributed here also to the retardation of humanity's progress.

To sum up, war is a selection for the worse, which destroys the more cultivated and leaves the more barbarous. It has always held back mental progress, and at this very day it increases mental stagnation. So I do not see how it can "ennoble" our kind by preventing us from "falling into dangerous lethargy.

CHAPTER VIII

MORAL EFFECTS

THE apologists of war extol its moral benefits above any of the others.

"Peace would produce corruption," says De Vogüé. Mr. Valbert is more explicit: " In peace man belongs to himself. He knows no other law than his personal interest. He no longer has any other occupation than to seek his own good. The greatest virtue is self-abnegation, the spirit of self-sacrifice, and it is in armies during war that that virtue is practised. It is not only the individuals whom war ennobles, but also the entire nation."[1]

---

[1] *Ibid.*, p. 696. The motive dictating these words is perfectly comprehensible. There are individuals in

69

WAR

Errors so manifest cannot be maintained except by the one-sided fallacy. Let us take the assailant's point of view. As a matter of fact, it is always the assailant who must be considered, since without attack there is no need for defence. As soon as we do this, the falsity of Mr. Valbert's proposition becomes apparent.

Say to a nation : " Arm yourselves to your teeth. Invade the country of your peaceful neighbours. Murder a goodly number of them on the battlefield. Then, after having conquered them, seize booty,

France who from sheer epicureanism would be quite willing to give up Alsace-Lorraine. They say : " Provided we have a good dinner and all sorts of pleasure, nothing else counts for much." All the dithyrambs in favour of war are a reaction against such tendencies. I am entirely of the same opinion as Mr. Valbert. If those dastards were to triumph, if France gave up Alsace-Lorraine, she would soon share Poland's fate. The French (and all other people) should vindicate their rights with their last drop of blood. So, what I write does not refer to those who defend their rights, but to those who violate the rights of others, in this case, not the French, but the Prussians.

impose heavy tributes, confiscate their lands, lay hold of the revenues from their taxes, live like parasites on the product of their toil. If the vanquished speak a language different from your own, stunt their intellectual development by the most violent despotism. If your new subjects profess a religion different from your own, treat them with intolerance. Deprive the heterodox of their civil and political rights, inflict the severest trials upon them, expel them *en masse*. Then we shall see all the virtues flourish in your midst, self-abnegation and the spirit of self-sacrifice. You will be regenerated and ennobled."

Who would venture to uphold a proposition so paradoxical? All the acts I just mentioned are the consequence of war. How can robbery, parasitism, intolerance, despotism, ennoble communities? How can the practice of those crimes develop all the virtues?

WAR

Let us abandon metaphysics and *a priori* reasoning. Let us use the empirical method in regard to social phenomena, just as it has been used for so many years in regard to physical phenomena. If war ennobles, then the most warlike nations should be the most moral, the peaceful nations the most corrupt. Do facts confirm that proposition ? Nowhere and never. From 1494 to 1559 almost constant warfare reddened Italy with blood. Do we find, as a result, that all the virtues flourished there ? On the contrary, immorality and licentiousness assumed more dreadful proportions than ever. It was then that such monsters as Pope Alexander VI. and his noble son Cæsar Borgia lived. Those wars and the awful anarchy that resulted from them degraded the Italian character to so low a level that more than two centuries were needed for dignity, magnanimity, and love of country to reassert themselves in even a slight degree. That is how war ennobles the nations. In the Orient the same causes produced the same effects. In the eighteenth century India was in a state similar to that of Italy in the sixteenth century. It was divided into a number of principalities, the chiefs of which had no other concern than to increase their territory. Complete anarchy prevailed. There were perpetual wars, and military expeditions for spoil were an organised industry. According to Mr. Valbert, India must have presented the spectacle of all the virtues. Alas ! with all due respect to Mr. Valbert, it was, on the contrary, a sink of all the vices. Indian society had been so corrupted by the ceaseless wars that, after a hundred years of the wise, healing administration of the English, scarcely any individuals out of a population of 287,000,000 to-day possess the feeling of honour or loyalty. Examples could be multiplied. What happened in

India has also taken place in other countries in similar circumstances.

Now, as to the effect of peace. There are four European nations which have completely renounced the idea of conquest on the European continent: the English, the Dutch, the Belgians, and the Swiss. Since they no longer think of conducting offensive warfare, they are absolutely pacific. According to Mr. Valbert and those who believe like him, they should constitute the scum of humanity. But with all due regard to the gentlemen, the very reverse is the case. The Swiss even offer an extreme example in proof of this. In the sixteenth century no war took place in the Occident without the participation of the Swiss. They were the most bellicose people of Europe. Everybody knows they were also the most corrupt.

Let us now take up another of Mr. Valbert's propositions. "War gives communities salutary instruction. A great German moralist defined war as ' a cure by iron which strengthens humanity,' and through the generosity of fate, this cure is more beneficial to the conquered than to the conquerors, who, infatuated by their glory, readily imagine that everything is permissible and possible to them."

Here again Mr. Valbert falls into the mistake of one-sided reasoning, which is all the more curious, since he himself notes it.

If a nation undergoes a defeat, another nation, necessarily, carries off a victory. If war regenerates the first, it corrupts the second. So the devil loses nothing. Sedan obliged the French " to pass judgment upon themselves, to see themselves as they are, to reproach themselves for their mistakes, to examine their own conscience, in order to prepare themselves for useful penitence and upliftment."[1] Jena produced the same effect upon Prussia. But, on the other hand, a result of Jena was to " infatuate " the French, and of Sedan to infatuate the Prussians. After 1806 we have a virtuous Prussia and a degenerate France. After 1871 we have a virtuous France and a degenerate Prussia. Where is the gain to humanity ?

But neither does the assertion that defeat always regenerates communities withstand criticism.[2] The Byzantine Empire attained the culmination of its power under Heraclius, who conducted a brilliant campaign against Persia. He penetrated to countries where the legions of Crassus and Trajan had never set foot. Soon after, the Arabs appeared. The Byzantines were beaten. At a stroke

---

[1] *Ibid.*, p. 696.

[2] Strange reasoning forsooth ! According to this we should always desire defeat. Sometimes after typhoid fever, it is said, a man feels better than he did before. Is that a reason for desiring typhoid fever ? It may regenerate, but, we forget, it often kills the patient.

they lost half their empire, all of Syria and Africa. Since that time until the taking of Constantinople by Mohammed II. the balance-sheet of the Byzantine wars shows a deficit. The Greeks of the Eastern Empire underwent frightful defeats. Has Greece been elevated on that account ? Has it given itself a better organisation ? Has it subjected itself to that self-examination which prepares them " for useful penitence and upliftment " ? We scarcely hear anything at all of Greece since the fall of the Eastern Empire.

The same may be said of the Turks. From John Sobieski to the present they have received the hardest lessons. It is difficult to count the number of battles in which they were soundly beaten. Nevertheless, the organisation of the Turkish Empire is as wretched to-day as it was in the seventeenth century ; in fact, in many respects more wretched. Then, where is

the " great upliftment " ? And Louis
XV.'s government, was it any better after
than before the battle of Rosbach ? Who
would venture to say it was ?

The truth is, certain nations rise after a
defeat as others continue to progress after a
victory—a fact depending upon extremely
numerous and complex causes which it
is impossible to enter into in this short
work. Sometimes defeat may be a factor
of progress, but it is very foolish and
superficial reasoning to attribute the
upliftment of nations to war alone.

The apologists of bloodshed forget a
further extremely important fact. There
are not only partial defeats, but also total
defeats. In 1856 Russia lost 1/1840 of
her territory, in 1871 France 1/38 of
hers. Those wounds were bearable.
Regeneration was possible. But the
Greek nation passed entirely under the
Ottoman yoke ; the Irish, under the
English yoke. The whole of Poland was

divided among its three neighbours. Now, as has long been admitted, political servitude develops the greatest defects in the subjugated peoples—hypocrisy, treachery, mendacity, baseness. The Bengalis, whom we discussed in Chapter II, were completely corrupted as a result of the successive invasions of their country. If the upliftment of a few nations may be posted on the debit side of war's ledger, we must post the complete demoralisation of many other nations on the credit side, and the balance-sheet will certainly show a loss. The elevation of sentiments in humanity is equal to a sum X, from which the degradation produced by violence and tyranny, that is, by war, must be deducted. The subtraction is formidable.

After a conquest the selection for the worse continues to operate with redoubled energy. Upon this point Mr. Vaccaro speaks very discerningly. "The victor, to assure himself of the obedience of the vanquished, persecutes and maltreats them. He even executes the strongest, the bravest, and most indomitable, while he allows the weaker, the more cowardly, the more obedient to live. Since these, to the exclusion of the others, beget children, the sentiments of baseness and servility become fixed in the race."[1]

Here we note an illogicality to which the nations said to be civilised, unfortunately, are well accustomed. The subjugated people are scorned because of their vices, and because they are scorned they come to be hated. The Russians profess profound contempt for the Poles, similarly all Christians profess profound contempt for the unfortunate Jews. Nevertheless, there was so simple a way of not degrading them—to respect the independence of the Poles, and not to

[1] *La lutte pour l'existence dans l'humanité*, Paris, Chevalier-Maresq, 1892, p. 51.

refuse civil and political rights to the Jews. But no, for eighteen centuries we have been maltreating the Jews most barbarously. They have fallen into disgrace. We hate them for that, instead of hating ourselves for having disgraced them. What admirable logic ! To be angry with the victims and not with the executioners ; with the corrupted and not with the corrupters.

From Buddha's times to ours, we have preached a great deal on morality by book and by word of mouth. The precepts have always been formulated, as it were, in the active voice : " Thou shalt not kill, thou shalt not steal, thou shalt not commit adultery, etc." The moralists have always had in eye the man who performs an act ; not the man who is the object of that act ; which is wholly logical, since the conduct of the object is conditioned by the conduct of the performer. But as soon as international relations come into question, common sense disappears as by magic. War is collective murder. Nevertheless, it is overwhelmed with encomiums, wonderful virtues are attributed to it, solely because, thanks to an incomprehensible fallacy, only those nations are had in mind which are the victims of attack, not those which commit them. We willingly concede to the apologists of war that to defend one's rights at the risk of one's life, or even to lose one's life in doing so, is the most admirable conduct imaginable. My warmest sympathy goes out to those noble victims who preferred death to disgrace. Yes, war might produce morality, but on the one condition that communities could defend themselves without being attacked.

Another argument. If the 8,000 wars of the historic period could not make us moral, what chance is there that the eight thousand and first will effect that result?

Can the apologists of war deny that

bloodshed produces international hatred, and international hatred produces the most baleful evils? Does it not set the greatest obstacle in the way of a mixture of races and the propagation of ideas? Is it not the most active cause of our backwardness and mental stagnation? Is it not war that has turned Europe into an intrenched camp and a mine of dynamite? Is it not war that has plunged us into the sad state in which we are to-day? "Too much gall has gathered among the European nations for them to be able to think of disarmament," says the *Moscow Gazette*.

Such reasoning is really remarkable. According to the Moscow journalist, disarmament is impossible because a new war is inevitable. It will be the cruellest war that history has ever noted in its annals, the horrible encounter of 12,000,000 men, armed with the most powerful engines of destruction. The victims will be numberless. If hostilities continue only a few months it will be by the hundreds of thousands that they will have to be counted.

But no matter how awful the carnage, there will be conquerors and conquered. The latter will nurse vengeance in their hearts. Does the Moscow journalist seriously think that after the hideous butchery of the future war, passions will by an incomprehensible miracle subside for ever ? No, they will be livelier than ever. After each defeat hatred becomes stronger and more bitter. The Germans have not forgotten the burning of the Palatinate. Then what is the meaning of the sentence, " Too much gall has gathered to permit disarmament " ? Ten times as much gall will gather after another war, crueller than all preceding. What sort of a future do the conservatives dream of ? Pitiless, endless bloodshed ? And is it by blood-shed that they count upon regenerating

the human race and making it moral ?
As well count upon petroleum to extin-
guish a conflagration.

To sum up, war, an appeal to brute
force, is always a degradation, a descent
into the animalism that demoralises the
victors, as well as the vanquished.

CHAPTER IX

IT is necessary to kill a living being for food, and man has had to make war upon plants and animals. Sometimes, when those sources of supply failed him he attacked his own kind, and practised cannibalism. Sometimes, too, he had to kill in order not to be eaten himself, and he therefore conducted long wars of extermination against animals to whom he might serve as prey. During the period of the struggle for food massacre is indispensable, since it is the very aim and purpose of the fight. Now, that period lasted hundreds of thousands of years, during which man grew accustomed to think of killing as the one procedure of fight.

Later, when foodstuffs became more abundant as a result of cattle-raising and agriculture, man began to covet the possessions of his neighbours. From that time date our economic and political wars, the razzias, the permanent tributes, the conquests. Because from the remotest periods man was accustomed to procure food by war, he thought war the quickest and most effective way of increasing his wealth. The day came when needs of an intellectual sort asserted themselves, and since all men could not think alike, differences of opinion arose. As a result of an acquired habit, they fancied that massacre was the best means of conversion, as they had thought it the best means of obtaining food.

We no longer share the delusions of our coarse ancestors. We know war does not enrich the victors, we know we can-

not work on man's conscience by material
means, we know that in order to combat
an opinion we must set up another
opinion in opposition to it. We know
all that, but alas! the ancient ideas im-
bedded in our brains for long generations
are not easily uprooted. The inefficacy
of war for settling economic, political and
spiritual questions is evident ; but we per-
sist in our timeworn ways, and continue
from tradition to use that method.

In reality the civilised peoples to-day
conduct wars simply because their savage
ancestors did so of old. There is no other
reason. It is a case of pure atavism, a
survival, a routine. From sheer spiritual
laziness they will not abandon their
accustomed habits. Then, because the
idea of carrying on war without any
motive is revolting to them, they erect
theory on theory, system on system to
justify it.

With war it is the same as with the

classic languages. Latin used to be the literary and scientific instrument of Europe. People learned it for the same reason that a Celt in Brittany now learns French. Greek literature contained a mine of delights and scientific information. In the fifteenth century Greek was studied for the same reason that a Russian to-day studies French. All that is past, but the routine remains. Averse to change our old methods of instruction, we have tried to justify them by the most extraordinary sophistries. Thus, one fine day, we discovered that the study of Greek and Latin is an excellent intellectual exercise, that it developed the reasoning faculty, and is a powerful instrument of culture. Of old, Greek and Latin were means to an end. As soon as they ceased to fulfil that function, they were raised to the dignity of ends in themselves.

The same in the case of war. For centuries men waged war to acquire wealth and honour. When it became evident that war impoverished the victors as well as the vanquished, the most remarkable virtues were ascribed to it. Sophistries fairly rained down—war makes nations moral, bloodshed prevents intellectual stagnation, and so on. It is noteworthy that all the benefits attributed to war were discovered after the event, exactly when public opinion turned away from it. The very same thing happened as with Latin. When the study of Latin became superfluous, its magical virtues were discovered.

Thus, these sophistries ring hollow and so can ill resist criticism.

War is analogous to crime, and crime is a desire become a passion, which does not recoil even before murder. If crime is an evil, why should war be a good ? Murder is war between individuals. Unfortunately, private murder, it is to be feared, will never cease. But no one extols it, no one discovers in it a means for making people moral. Similarly, civil wars are not recommended, though they, too, are inevitable. It is simply in the case of the foreigner that massacre is productive of all its virtues. But that word foreigner is absolutely conventional. In the fourteenth century the inhabitants of the 650 States of Germany considered one another foreigners. A prince had two sons, and divided his realm between them. Thenceforward the subjects of the elder became *foreigners* to the subjects of the younger. If the prince had had only one son, they would have remained compatriots. Then, how can collective murder be rendered beneficial by a mere chance of succession ? Of old, the Germans of Austria, the Czechs, and the Magyars regarded one another as foreigners. In 1526 Ferdinand I. was selected king of Bohemia and Hungary, and forthwith those races became fellow-countrymen. To-day the French and the

English are foreigners to each other. If to-morrow it would please them to form a political union, they would instantly become compatriots. Do differences in language make foreigners ? If so, a Breton would not be a Frenchman. There is not a single great State in Europe in which several languages are not spoken, languages sometimes widely remote in origin from one another, like the Basque and the Spanish. The Basque is not even an Aryan tongue. There is more kinship between Spanish and Russian than between Spanish and Basque. This example shows that various languages may be spoken without the compulsion arising for men to fall upon one another like wild beasts.

I repeat, the word foreigner is purely conventional, and when the apologists of war assert that war produces all the virtues because it is waged against the foreigner, I ask, then, first of all for an absolutely clear and precise definition of that word.

SURVIVALS AND SOPHISTRIES

With war it is the same as with another fallacy of the human mind, protection. If duties increase wealth, why not establish them, for example, between New York and Pennsylvania just as they are established between New York and Germany? Similarly, if war is beneficial, if it "gives men the opportunity to perform feats of heroism, self-denial, and devotion," why not wage war between subjects of the same country? Civil war can develop all those virtues as well as international war.

Now let us consider the sophistries of the apologists of bloodshed from a strictly moral point of view.

Folly, crime, and vice exist. Therefore, they "conform to the order of things established by God," as Von Moltke said. Nevertheless, nobody delights in, nobody honours, and nobody covers with blessings folly, crime, and vice. Nobody tries to prove that they maintain the human virtues. On the contrary, people try to fight them down in every conceivable way. X does not succeed in convincing Y. He attacks Y, and kills him. We consider that act hideous so long as it occurs between individuals. But if it were a collective act, we should fall into a delirium of admiration. What enthusiasm the crusades of the Spaniards against the Mohammedans arouse in us!

War, the apologists say, evokes heroism and great devotion. They do not perceive, in arguing in that way, that the necessity for heroism, like the necessity for charity, is highly regrettable. It would be a thousand times better if all men were rich and provident and never had need of help. Who would be so silly as to recommend that each year several thousand individuals be ruined in order that saintly charity should have the opportunity to perform its admirable ministrations? Has any one ever recommended that cholera or diphtheria germs be spread so that physicians should have the chance to give proof of their devotion to humanity? What fool would suggest that a few hundred houses be set on fire every year for the firemen to be able to show their heroism and not let that virtue atrophy among them?

Those compassionate persons who deprive themselves of many joys to help their fellow-men, the Sisters of Charity, the physicians, the firemen, who save the lives of others by sometimes sacrificing their own, deserve our liveliest gratitude and admiration. But we should wish that they never had the occasion to perform their services. For a long time we have been doing everything to render their work needless. This line of argument unqualifiedly applies to war. The soldier who dies for his country commits a most praiseworthy deed. But we should wish that he never had the opportunity to do so. To preach war in order to secure that opportunity to him is folly, pure and simple.

Another virtue has been attributed to war, that of preventing over-population. Of all the sophistries this is the most upside-down. A woman brings a child into the world, suckles him at her breast, rears him in love. He receives a good education, to defray the expenses of which his family does its utmost. At the age of twenty-one he and the other finest young men of the generation are chosen for war and sent to be butchered in order to prevent over-population. Is not that pure madness? If we actually were suffering from over-population, would it not be better to abstain from having children than to kill off the flower of each generation in that barbarous fashion?

Some years ago, anarchists threw bombs in several European cities. They said they were angry at our rotten society and would regenerate it with dynamite. What chiefly outraged the world in their savage deeds is the fact that innocent persons were injured. But war has always had the same effect.

Napoleon III., his satellites, his low, servile legislature were corruption personified. According to Mr. Jähns, Mr. Valbert, and their like, Sedan was a means of regenerating all of them.[1] But, alas! how many thousands of victims, the bravest men in the land, fell in that battle! Peasants who had worked from morning to evening, good fathers who had loved their children, who had economised every penny, and had prepared the true greatness of the country. The vulgar herd of courtiers, who had instigated the butcheries, suffered no harm, and after the signing of the peace they again took up their life of pleasure and dissipation. That is how

---

[1] Upon the mere formulation of such a statement we see its absolute fallaciousness.

WAR

war makes the people moral. It sacrifices the innocent, and spares the culpable. If the apologists of bloodshed find this means efficacious, we congratulate them upon it with perfect sincerity.

According to Mr. Valbert, if it depended upon a moralist to suppress war, he might hesitate perhaps. Strange! Why not say the same of plagues, epidemics, cholera, earthquakes, cyclones, droughts? There is not a man alive in his good senses, the most ordinary man, who would not, if he could, suppress all those evils at one blow. War is the privileged plague. While we curse the others, we bless war and find great virtues in it. When nature destroys men and wealth, we deem it a calamity. When men rabidly annihilate and impoverish one another we deem it a fortunate event. The reader may say I am obtuse, but I frankly admit I am utterly incapable of grasping that point of view. It is the same with war as with protection. When high prices are natural they are an evil, and everything is done to fight them. Roads, canals, railroads, and machines of every sort are constructed. But when high prices are artificially produced by customs duties, they are considered good.

Let any one who wishes explain such curious logic. As for myself, I am completely at a loss. With my natural candour I aver I have a very individual way of regarding the plagues that torment humanity. We may call upon the earth not to quake, the volcanoes not to belch their lava, the winds not to blow away the fertilising rain-clouds. But to what purpose? Cruel nature is deaf to our adjurations. So we bow our heads and patiently endure the inevitable scourges. But when scourges are produced by creatures endowed with reason, who could perfectly well prevent the infliction of them, I can only feel thoroughly indignant and disgusted. Yes, forsooth, war deserves a privileged place among the plagues that torment humanity, but a place at the very opposite end from the one it has been assigned. It should be a hundred times more execrated than drought, or cholera, or tuberculosis, because on the very day we take measures to suppress it, it will disappear.

Civil law punishes instigation to murder. Those who vaunt the benefits of war instigate to murder. Without doubt, they do so in good faith, and we do not ask the law to punish them. But they are vicious persons and should be pinned in the pillory of public opinion, exposed to execration and shame.

CHAPTER X

THE PSYCHOLOGY OF WAR

THE external world produces sensations in us which in our nerve-centres turn into perceptions, images, ideas, sentiments, desires, and passions. When the phase of desire is reached, an action generally takes place. In the phase of desire the mind is for a time still master of itself. It chooses its means, takes present attendant circumstances into consideration (for instance, the interests of human beings), or future circumstances anticipated. But if the external sensation reaches the phase of passion, the mind is carried away completely and annuls all resistance. Then man, in order to realise a desired end, recoils before no means, not even the sacrifice of his fellow-beings. To kill is both an individual and a collective act—in the first case being called murder ; in the second, war.

There are three critical moments in a murder—the desire, whatever it may be ; the conviction that the desire can be realised only by a man's death, and the accomplishment of the deed.

The same phases exist in collective murder—a lust for something enkindled in a group (the desire to acquire wealth, land, honours, and so on), the conviction that the end desired can be attained only by battles, and, finally, the commencement of hostilities.

But in collective murder matters are considerably complicated. Each man at each instant has his own special desires.

To produce an act in common those desires must be co-ordinated. Hence the initiative of an individual is indispensable to the origin of every collective act. A man conceives an undertaking for spoliation. He looks about for companions to help him. He becomes the head of a band and recruits troops for a military expedition. During a certain phase of society war is always a private affair.

But how is it that the chief always finds companions? Every living creature dreads death. How is it that persons will expose themselves to it quite willingly? Here another factor enters—hope. Each person before a fight knows that inevitably some will fall, even among the victors. But who will fall? Each man thinks his fellows will, not himself, and so enlists under the standard of the chief. In other words, he does not sacrifice his life, but risks it for the sake of obtaining certain advantages. If volunteers were all as certain of being killed as a convict is of being executed, the number of wars would be infinitely less.

When the modern States were organised and the standing armies established, wars ceased to be private enterprises. The right to declare war became the monopoly of the Governments.

Far-reaching changes then took place in the play of interests. The soldier who had quite voluntarily enrolled under a chief's standard had had the consciousness of advantages to be derived from doing so. He sometimes stipulated in advance what the advantages should be. But when war came to be monopolised by the heads of a State, the advantages to a soldier ceased to be apparent.[1] To get

[1] Because they no longer exist in reality. Some individuals may derive benefits from a war, but entire nations never. On this point see my *Gaspillages*, chapter xiii.

men to decide to fight it is necessary to employ an amount of complex measures which Tolstoy very accurately describes as the hypnotisation of the masses. A number of institutions—the Church, the school, and many others—lay hold of a man when he leaves the cradle, and impress certain special ideas upon him. He is made to believe that it is to his interest to be ready at any moment to throw himself upon his fellow-beings and massacre them. He is made to believe that his happiness is in direct ratio to the size of the State. One of the most effectual ways of keeping up the military spirit is to represent to people that they are always on the defensive and their neighbours alone are aggressors. That illusion has taken hold of all the nations.

A few examples :—Several years ago an anonymous writer very clearly showed the French point of view in an article in

WAR

the *Revue des Deux Mondes* of February 1,
1894, *La paix armée et ses conséquences.*
" In 1863," the writer says, " Europe was
happy. It seemed to be on the eve
of the era of international fraternity.
People saw the time when all the nations
of Europe would vow unalterable affec-
tion for one another. The state of
things was truly idyllic.[1] But Bismarck
appeared ! He treacherously attacked
Denmark, next Austria, and finally
France. Then Europe became an armed
camp, a mine of dynamite. Farewell to
the beautiful dreams of love ! Farewell
to the idyll ! Prussia, whose ' national
industry is war,' was the great disturber
of peace, the great criminal."

---

[1] One fact will show how fanciful this picture is. At
that time a number of French patriots were dreaming
of the conquest of the Rhine frontier lands. Germany and Belgium were living in a state of perpetual
fright. The hegemony of France under Napoleon III.
weighed as heavily as that of Prussia to-day.

Let us cross the Rhine into Germany. Here we hear a different tune. "We Germans are the most peaceable people in the world. We do not want to take anybody's land [except Alsace-Lorraine]. If it depended upon us, Europe would be enjoying absolute peace. But, then, there's the Gallic Cock and the Russian Bear. Neither will keep quiet, and we are forced every year to equip new regiments." Some time ago a German author showed that France was the eternal obstacle to disarmament, and he proposed to divide it into several States forming a federation.[1] In that event alone could our unfortunate continent finally draw its breath in peace.

The author of a pamphlet published in

---

[1] The clever journalist forgets "to light his lantern," like the monkey in the fable. He does not once stop to consider whether the French would consent to such a combination.

WAR

Germany[1] asks if peace is possible in Europe so long as a Russia exists. Many Germans declare that in order to obtain peace the barbarous Muscovites must be thrust back to the steppes of Siberia.[2]

Now let us cross the Niemen. "We are gentleness personified," say the Russians. "But the road to Constantinople leads through Berlin. Germany prevents us from accomplishing our historic mission. Through sheer jealousy it thwarts the realisation of our national programme, and infringes upon our most sacred rights. It is Germany that attacks—we merely defend ourselves."

Thus, everywhere we see the same thing. Each nation imagines itself to be

---

[1] *Was will das Volk? Weder Krieg noch Militarismus.*

[2] To obtain this result it would be necessary to form a European federation without Russia. The Germans, we must realise, would hardly take that step.

the personification of virtue. Each nation, as Mr. Jähns would have it, pretends it wages none but defensive wars.

It is time to eradicate such fatal errors. The great European nations should subject their consciences to a severe examination. They would then perceive that they are all equally violent and equally brutal.[1] The policy of each one of them prevents the happiness of millions of human beings.

No, our neighbour is not the sole aggressor. We, too, are aggressors. It is not true that we confine ourselves to self-defence. No, we violate the rights of others, just as others violate our rights.

When these truths will have pene-

[1] Except France *at present.* In demanding a plebiscite in Alsace-Lorraine the French merely upheld their rights and made no attacks upon the rights of anyone else.

trated into the minds of the masses, militarism will have seen its last days. At present, in fact, war can possess advantages—I refer, also, even to purely imaginary advantages—for only a very small number of individuals. If the masses agree to wage war, it is because they think it is simply a defensive war. Dispel that illusion, and no one would go to battle.

The people hate war. There is not a man in ten thousand who would willingly, for pleasure, enter a campaign. This has always been so. To be sure, the Romans may be considered to have been a warlike nation. Augustus was the first to close the Temple of Janus. But even in the time of the Republic the *vacatio militaris* (exemption from military service) was granted as a reward. Beginning with Marius, conscription (*dilectus*) had to be given up. The rich refused to serve. So, we see, war was dreaded even by the most warlike people on earth. In the early Middle Ages all free men were soldiers. But, it seems, that did not greatly amuse them, because after the fifteenth century standing armies had to be created. If war had been a pleasure, men would have been enthusiastic to rally about the royal standards. That such was not the case is evident from the fact that conscription was introduced.

As for modern times, it may be stated without fear of error that from the Ural Mountains to the Atlantic the Europeans have the utmost horror of conscription and war. Nobody would consent to be a soldier if he were not certain of being punished for refusing to serve. It is less vexatious to be a soldier in England than anywhere else; yet, since the Crimean War, " the average number of deserters from the English Army has never been less than one-fifth of the recruits. Sometimes as many as one-half have deserted."[1]

No person on awaking in the morning thinks of going to break his fellow-men's heads. A man merely tries to increase his prosperity according to his ability. I can give material proof of this. Have we ever seen a people petition for war? They accept it because they think it inevitable, but they always go against their will.

Thanks to the perfected organisation of modern societies, an order emanating from the Cabinet can in a few hours set a nation of 100,000,000 souls astir. Sometimes orders are given odious to the great majority of citizens, who nevertheless obey them as a result of social reflexes. The custom of obeying the Head of the

[1] E. Reclus, *Nouvelle géographie universelle*, vol. iii, p. 881.

State has become so much a matter of second nature that the idea of resistance has completely disappeared.

The social organisation permits certain individuals, very few in number, to decide the fate of the largest States. To obtain material advantages or to satisfy their self-love, those individuals sometimes bring about the bloodiest wars. Assuredly the French never had a thought of making the expedition into Russia in 1812.[1] But Napoleon wanted it. The German producers and labourers certainly never thought of invading France in 1870. But the three boon companions—Moltke, Von Roon, and Bismarck—wanted to invade France.

A happy combination of circumstances has been produced and still exists.

[1] The intention to wage this war was kept a secret. When the emperor left Paris to begin the campaign, the *Moniteur* merely announced that he was going to inspect the *Grande Armée*, then assembled at the Vistula.

WAR

No minister is great enough to create his own policy. The monarchs of the large European nations are too imbued with humanitarian sentiments to start the most awful wars in order to experience some of those delicious emotions that victory bestows. None of them is selfish enough to inflict horrible sufferings upon millions of human beings for the satisfaction of self-love.[1]

Since neither the people nor the monarchs desire war, it would seem that the nations could disarm and form the United States of Europe. Why do they not? There is only one reason, but that a powerful one—ROUTINE, convention.

This, I know, will seem paradoxical to many of my readers. But it is upon

[1] Emperor William II. said to Jules Simon in March, 1890 : " Your army is prepared. It has made great progress. . . . That is why I should regard any one who would drive the two nations to war as a simpleton or a criminal.

mature reflection that I am led to this conclusion, and I think, sooner or later, it will be accepted by all enlightened minds.

Yes, alas ! War will be waged in the future simply because it was waged in the past. The future battles of the Europeans will be frightful holocausts offered to SAINT ROUTINE.

At present many questions are still undecided. But every man endowed with ordinary common sense understands perfectly well that they can be settled without the least difficulty by arbitration or the plebiscite. If we reject these means and prefer battle, we do so, I repeat, for only one reason—because in the same circumstances our ancestors declared war, and we have to do the same that they did. Our ancestors considered it shameful to give a country its independence without shedding blood. So we must also consider it

WAR

shameful. A still small voice cries to us
from every corner that it is not shameful,
that the oppression of foreign nations is
shameful, base, contrary to our interests.
Yet we stifle that blessed voice of healthy
reason to listen to the voice of our preferred fetich, SAINT ROUTINE.

CHAPTER XI

WAR CONSIDERED AS THE SOLE
FORM OF STRUGGLE

THE apologists of war are quite right in this—that struggle is life. Struggle is the action of the environment upon the organism and the reaction of the organism upon the environment, therefore a perpetual combat. Absolute peace would be the suppression of that motion : that is, it would be a pure abstraction, since matter is one and the same thing as motion, or dynamics, and we distinguish between them by a subjective operation of the mind.

Man will cease to struggle the day his

desires cease, which is tantamount to saying the day he dies. As soon as conflict stops, stagnation and death set in. " Cemeteries are really the one place in the world where perpetual peace reigns." [1]

Without struggle and antagonism, societies would indeed fall into a state of somnolency, of most dangerous lethargy. That is perfectly true, but the great mistake consists in considering war the sole form in which humanity's struggle manifests itself.

Confusions of the same sort are numerous. The most eminent philosophers declare that some day the universe will reach absolute equilibrium. That state of things is represented as the absence of all motion. Now, equilibrium merely signifies constancy of the trajectories. If tomorrow the earth began to revolve at the rate of 50 kilometres a second, the day

[1] Valbert, *ibid.*, p. 692.

after at the rate of 10 kilometres, and the third day at the rate of 100 kilometres, the solar system would be in a state of non-equilibrium. But if it continues to revolve with its normal velocity of 29 kilometres per second, the system remains in equilibrium. Equilibrium may be a quality of any degree of velocity, no matter how great.

Similarly, the most heated conflicts may agitate humanity. Activity, feverish doings may go on everywhere all the time, every moment of the day, and yet it is unnecessary for men to kill one another on fields of battle, like wild beasts. It is easy to demonstrate that the intensity of motion would be in direct ratio to the infrequency of bloodshed. In fact, war produces anarchy and disorder, which bring on intellectual stagnation, and intellectual stagnation is the minimum of cerebral motion, or cerebral dynamics. In a state of order and justice—that is, in a state of peace—the mind soars on its highest flights ; which means that the velocity of cerebral action increases.

The main error, then, arises in a confusion of war with struggle, whereas war is merely a means, a procedure for attaining certain ends.   Now, this truth long ago took form in customary modes of expression, in which the loftiest intellectual speculations of a given community manifest themselves.

I shall take a few phrases at random, the first my eyes fall upon. " When Mr. Casimir-Perier descends from the tribune, the Government will have won the battle, and Mr. Millerand will enter only to cover the retreat." [1]   Speaking of the government of the Radicals, Mr. de Marcère says that " it produced in the relations between the citizens and the State, or between the representatives of the

[1] *Journal des Débats,* May 9, 1894.

State and the citizens, and even among families, a condition of intestine war and an unwillingness to make mutual concessions, which caused France to resemble a multitude of hostile camps." [1]   Recently Mr. Philippe Gill published a book entitled *La bataille littéraire* (" The Literary Battle "). " Each chapter deals with one of the forms of the struggle in which we take part—the fight of the idealists against the naturalists, the fight of the spiritualists against the romanticists, of paradox against reason." [2]   The reader knows without my saying so that in all the contests mentioned in these quotations not a single drop of blood was shed.

Twenty times a day we use similar expressions.   What does that show ? Simply that the wisdom of the nations long ago discovered the elementary truth

[1] *Nouvelle Revue*, May 1, 1894, p. 8.
[2] *Ibid.*, May 15, 1894, p. 452.

that war aiming at the conquest of
territory is not the sole form of struggle
in human groups. It takes on a great
number of other forms. But, the reader
will say, your axiom is the asses' bridge.
Exactly. That is the very point I
wish to reach. Is it not strange that
so simple an idea, one so widely spread,
should not have struck the apologists of
war?

The idea of diversity · in struggle is
as trite as the idea of the division of
labour. Division of labour began in the
remotest periods, in the age of stone, when
man went hunting and marauding, and
woman cooked. Besides, man need
merely look upon his own body to see
division of labour practised on an immense
scale. The hands and feet perform
distinctly different functions. The ears
cannot see, nor the eyes hear. All that
should be suggestive, should it not?

Nevertheless, the first thinker who realised the importance of division of labour and studied it scientifically was Adam Smith in the second half of the eighteenth century. Thus, a fact observed thousands and thousands of times in the course of ages was not fully comprehended and did not become part of our conscious thought until the year 1776 of our era.

Man is a very complex being. He feels the need for food, the desire to reproduce, he feels economic, political, intellectual and moral needs. Each of these needs impels him to act. When he encounters resistance, arising either from his physical environment or from causes of a different sort, or from his fellow-men, he feels like overcoming them. To do so most rapidly and effectually, the employment of different methods is expedient— work, violence, persuasion, etc.

WAR

Now, the routine thinkers of the school of Mr. Jähns and Mr. Valbert do not understand that elementary truth. They fancy that the one struggle there is in society aims at the annexation of one's neighbour's lands, and that the sole method of fighting is to murder on battlefields.

Such narrow-mindedness is all the more astonishing in the French author, because his country is now a centre of extremely heated contests which are not carried on by the method of butchery. In the first place, there is the economic struggle, which Socialism has made so serious. Then there is the conflict of free thought with the Catholic Church, which assumed so acute a form under the Radical Government. Finally, there is the question of assimilating the 12,000,000 Languedocians, Flemings, Celts, etc., with the dominant nationality. In Algeria, besides, the

AS SOLE FORM OF STRUGGLE

French are striving to Gallicise the Arabs. How is it that Mr. Valbert does not see all those facts?

Conquest, then, is not the sole object of struggle, and war is not the one method. It may even be said that war, or murder, is not really effectual except in the physiological, or food, struggle. X is hungry. He can find no food. He throws himself upon Y and kills and eats him. That is a cruel but a rational act. If we did not wage war upon the vegetables and animals, if we did not murder them, it would be impossible for us to live. But once the physiologic stage has been past, war is an ineffectual method. The economic struggle has wealth for its object. As soon as war is employed, so far from increasing we diminish wealth. The aim of the intellectual struggle is to lead other men to think like myself. As soon as war

is used as a method of conviction, so far
from hastening we retard the spread of
ideas.[1]

When the idea of the diversity of
social struggles will have formed part
of our conscious thought, when it will
have become public property, men will
be amazed to see how it remained unrecognised so long. Alas ! the asses'
bridges are sometimes the hardest to cross.
We may say that all scientific endeavour
is directed toward bringing certain truths
to be classed among those of the celebrated
Monsieur de La Palisse.

> La Palisse lacked prosperity,
>   He barely kept alive.
> But when he had things in plenty,
>   He then began to thrive.

That seems undeniable, does it not ? I
shall proceed to present to the reader

[1] The limitations of the present work do not allow of
the elaboration of this point. I refer the reader to my
Luttes entre sociétés humaines.

another, still more amazing truth, also unrecognised for thousands of years and still denied by a very large number of people, " wealth cannot be increased by being destroyed." Most assuredly Monsieur de La Palisse would turn in his grave if he heard this. As I showed in a previous chapter, within historic times man destroyed the value of £160,000,000,000, always in the delusion that the destruction would increase his wealth. If men were only to regulate their conduct according to La Palisse's truth, that wealth cannot be increased by destroying it, nobody would again wage a war of conquest, since men would understand that wars impoverish the victors as well as the vanquished. When will that happy moment come ?

The same conditions prevail in the other human struggles. They have many objects, and the effectualness of methods of fighting vary according to the end in view. When men adjust their conduct to that elementary truth, the face of the world will be completely changed.

CHAPTER XII

THE THEORISTS OF BRUTE FORCE

DARWIN's genius produced a profound revolution in all the sciences. A veil fell from before our eyes. Facts observed for centuries over and over again were for the first time interpreted in a scientific way. We saw that each tree, each blade of grass fights with its neighbour for the nourishing elements of the earth and the sun's light. We realised that each insect, each animal can live only by destroying other living beings. The idea of struggle was soon transferred from biologic phenomena to all others. We saw that struggle was the universal law of nature. Atoms contend with one another to form chemical

129 K

substances. The nebulæ and the stars vie for the matter spread in the celestial spheres. The cells of our body are engaged without cease in a furious conflict. The ideas in our brain struggle for ascendancy one over the other. In short, we find tension and effort, the manifestation of eternal energy, everywhere. Through Darwin our conception of the universe has been entirely changed. From something static it has become dynamic.

As every political reaction runs beyond its goal, so every new theory leads some minds too far in one direction. The truer it is, the more impetuous its current. It submerges everything. It prevents us from taking account of certain phenomena which are of the utmost importance.

Social phenomena are not absolutely identical with biologic phenomena. They present a number of new factors not to be neglected. Because massacre is the method most frequently employed in the struggles between animal species, it does not necessarily follow that it must be employed by the human species, too. Besides the physiological struggle, humanity has economic, political, and intellectual struggles, which do not exist among animals. It may even be stated that the physiological struggle, the dominant form in the animal kingdom, has ended among men, since they no longer eat one another.

This is something that certain theorists have not understood. Fascinated by the Darwinian ideas, they have accepted them blindly without perceiving the modifications they undergo in the social environment.

The " Origin of Species " was first published in 1859. A few years later, thanks to the appearance of the great political " genius," Bismarck, Europe underwent a period of comparative barbarisation. That narrow - minded Prussian provincial, stony-hearted and ambitious as Napoleon, adored nothing but brute force. He knew of no other way to fight than with the sword. He proclaimed that the bayonet exceeds the law, and that everything in the world should be accomplished by blood and iron. His prestige in Germany was immense. He was idolised like a demi-god. The tokens of servile adulation with which he was overwhelmed in his country show better than anything else the degradation of a vast number of the German people.

Darwin incorrectly interpreted on the one side, and Bismarck's prestige on the other, combined to produce a new school of theorists who have remade history after their fashion. In order to undertake an investigation, men must necessarily have a preconceived idea. As a result they see things not as they actually are, but as they would have them. That is why the confirmation of the oddest systems hatched by the most grotesque imaginations is read into history.

A professor of the University of Gratz, Mr. Gumplowicz, in 1883, published a work entitled *Der Rassenkampf* ("Race Wars"), in which the tendencies of the theorists of brute force are very clearly shown up. According to Mr. Gumplowicz, mankind has a polygenist origin. Each race comes from a distinct stock. Consequently, antagonism and hatred have always existed among the human races, and will continue to divide them to the end of time. "The perpetual struggle of the races is the law of history," Mr. Gumplowicz concludes, "while perpetual peace is nothing but the dream of the idealists." A disciple of his, Mr. Ratzenhofer, condenses his theory to

133

a single proposition, " The contact of two hordes produces rage and terror. They throw themselves upon one another in a fight to exterminate, or else they avoid contact."[1]

Until now it was believed that men fought their fellows in order to obtain food, women, wealth, the profits derived from the possession of the government, or in order to impose a religion or a type of culture. In all these circumstances war is a means to an end. The new theorists proclaim that this is all wrong. Men must of necessity massacre one another because of polygeny. Savage carnage is a law of nature, operating through FATALITY.

That is very fine. But let us see if these grim theories can hold their own when confronted with facts.

In 1865, 132 Welsh disembarked at

---

[1] *Wesen und Zweck der Politik*, Leipsic, Brockhaus, 1893, vol. i, p. 9.

Golfo Nuevo, in Patagonia. They set to work, but the crops were poor, and the little colony came near starving. " Fortunately, on their first meeting with the native Indians, the Tehuel-Che, they had entered into friendship with them, and the Indians gave them food, bringing them game, fish, and fruits in exchange for some small articles of English manufacture." [1] Can one imagine two more dissimilar races than the Celts from Wales and the Tehuel-Che of Patagonia ? And I ask Mr. Ratzenhofer how it is that upon their first meeting the two races did not throw themselves upon one another and fight " a fight to exterminate " ? I answer, because the alleged *fatality* of such a conflict is a purely metaphysical creation. Every living being pursues joy and not struggle. The contact of two hordes may

[1] E. Reclus, *Nouvelle géographie universelle*, vol. xix, p. 752.

produce the most dissimilar results, hostility as well as amity. That depends upon the interests involved and thousands of fortuitous circumstances.

If I were not afraid of wearying the reader, I should cite facts to prove that on numerous occasions the first contact of two very different races has been peaceful like that of the Welsh and the Tehuel-Che. It could not be otherwise. If the theories of Mr. Gumplowicz and Mr. Ratzenhofer were true, the very foundations of psychology would be overturned. We should have to concede that there are actions unaccompanied by volition. When man attacks a creature of his own or of a different kind, he always does so in obedience to a desire to acquire some good or defend himself against some evil. But the " fight to exterminate " of two hordes would be an act without an object, therefore a psychologic impossibility.

THEORISTS OF BRUTE FORCE

The mere appearance of an alien does not always constitute an injury in itself. Without doubt misoneism, the tendency to consider everything new as disagreeable, is undeniably a trait of human beings. But, on the other hand, the existence of philoneism, the very opposite tendency, is also not to be denied. It, too, is an essential trait. Monotony produces boredom, genuine suffering. The cases in which foreigners are well received are just as numerous as those in which they are not.

That is why, I must repeat, the contact of two social groups may produce the most unlike consequences, alliance as well as conflict. No grim FATALITY obliges us to massacre one another eternally like wild beasts. All the theories based on that alleged fatality are pure phantasmagorias absolutely devoid of all positive reality.

At this point I must bring up another

137

error which has been the cause of much abuse lately—the alleged race wars. They, too, are mere creations of the fancy. Until now there have been no race wars, for the simple reason that the races have not been conscious of their individuality. When the wars for political domination took place between two linguistic groups, they became race wars by chance. The Germans did not fight the Slavs on their eastern boundary because they hated them but in order to acquire territory which they coveted.[1] The French made conquests along the Rhine, not from hatred of the Germans, but to increase the size of their State. They fought the Spaniards for the same purpose, though the Spaniards, like themselves, are Latins.

---

[1] The wars Charlemagne waged against the Saxons were just as cruel as the wars of the Germans against the Slavs. Yet Charlemagne and the Saxons both belonged to the Teutonic race.

THEORISTS OF BRUTE FORCE

The idea of nationality, which is more concrete, is of very recent origin, that of race all the more so. The Slavs have had the consciousness of the unity of their race only since the works of Safarik and his emulators, that is, for only about sixty years. The Swedes, the Danes, and the Germans are Teutons. That has not prevented them from fighting one another furiously, and it did not impel them to adopt common institutions. Nothing is more conventional than the idea of race. Where can the boundary lines between races be drawn? We settle them arbitrarily from purely subjective considerations.[1] Hence, racial differences have had

[1] If the physiologic differences that divide a Frenchman from a German constitute the limits of a race, why should not the same hold for the physiologic differences between a Norman and a Provençal? They are just as great. But where draw the line? It may just as well be said that the Bavarians and the Prussians form different races. As a matter of fact, the boundaries do not exist in nature, but are pure subjective categories of our mind.

but a slight influence upon political history. The Arabs and Spaniards, it would seem, formed two quite distinct races between whom an alliance was impossible. Yet what do we find in fact? That the famous Cid Campeador, Spain's national hero, sometimes allied himself with Mohammedan emirs and fought *Christian* princes. The object of the wars in the Middle Ages was to obtain possession of as much territory as possible, and until the present time that has been the chief cause of wars. I challenge any one to cite a single campaign *consciously* undertaken for the purpose of upholding the interests of a race.

CHAPTER XIII

ANTAGONISM AND SOLIDARITY

HAPPILY the theories of Mr. Gumplowicz and Mr. Ratzenhofer are as false as they are unmerciful. At first man is guided by no incomprehensible FATALITY, but simply by his interests. Assuredly, a social group is not impelled to go massacre another social group because humanity has a polygenist origin. Little care I who my ancestor was a thousand generations ago. What I care about is to have the maximum of enjoyment with the minimum of work.

But what is more, the authors just mentioned have entirely neglected another side of the question. They have seen

conflict alone; they have not seen, or
have not laid stress upon, the phenomenon
of alliance. What sort of a chemist
would he be who merely saw the forces
driving chemical bodies apart and failed
to study those that produce cohesion?
These are the two sides of the same
phenomenon. The atoms cannot disappear from the universe. If they leave
one body, they must necessarily join
another. Chemistry is properly the
science of atomic *composites*. The same is
true of communities. Conflict and alliance are two simultaneous and parallel
phenomena characterising social groups.
"Let several murderers," says Mr.
Lacombe, "who have decided to war
upon society unite and form a union of
their own, there will soon be an expressed
[or tacit] agreement among them not to
kill one another."[1] In order that one

[1] *De l'histoire considérée comme science*, p. 77.

142

social group may undertake a fight against another, an alliance among the unities of which it is composed must necessarily be established.

Mr. Gumplowicz well knows that in the Quaternary Age hordes of several hundreds of persons composed the social group and fought against similar groups. In 1870, 38,000,000 Frenchmen fought an equal number of Germans. If the hordes had always " thrown themselves upon one another in a fight to exterminate," or if they had always " avoided contact," how could such immense associations as that ever have been organised ? In fact, the alliances among hordes, tribes, cities, and States have been just as numerous and frequent as conflicts. Always, when hostilities begin, allies are sought. History mentions as many coalitions of States as wars against them. To-day Europe is divided into two camps

—the triple alliance forming the one, France and Russia the other. Here, too, then, we see alliance going hand in hand with antagonism. Moreover, how is it that Mr. Gumplowicz does not see that association has no limits? Nothing would prevent 1,480,000,000 men inhabiting 135,000,000 square kilometres from forming an alliance to-morrow, just as nothing prevented 381,000,000 men inhabiting 25,000,000 square kilometres from forming one to-day.[1]

The Darwinian law in no wise prevents the whole of humanity from joining in a federation in which peace will reign.

But, you will say, how reconcile that with the perpetual struggle, which is the universal law of nature? The answer is simple. You need merely recollect that

[1] The first pair of numbers represent all the inhabitants of the globe and the extent of all the continents. The second, the population and the size of the British Empire.

massacre is not the sole form in which struggle manifests itself. Within the federation of humanity the same will take place as takes place within each State. Here struggle has by no means disappeared, but goes on under the form of economic competition, lawyers' briefs, judges' sentences, votes, party organisations, parliamentary discussions, meetings, lectures, sermons, schools, scientific associations, congresses, pamphlets, books, newspapers, magazines—in short, by spoken and written propaganda. And we must not suppose that these methods have been preferred to bloodshed because men have become better. Idylls play no part in this question. These methods have been preferred simply because they were found to be the most effective, therefore the quickest and easiest. " We shall not give you the satisfaction of shooting us down in the street," Liebknecht once said to

Count Caprivi. If the Socialists prefer
the vote as a fighting weapon, that is
most certainly not from love of the
Conservatives.

All the methods of struggle just
enumerated are constantly employed in
normal times among 381,000,000 of
English subjects inhabiting 25,000,000 of
square kilometres. They could be
equally well employed by 1,480,000,000
men inhabiting 135,000,000 square kilometres. Then the federation of the entire
globe would be achieved.

Why do we say that the French form a
political unity ? Simply because in normal
conditions they do not war with one
another. But does that mean that they
have given up the other methods of
struggle I mentioned ? Not at all. The
synthesis of antagonism and solidarity is
produced in the simplest fashion in the
world once people decide to cross the

asses' bridge and consciously decide to understand what language has already formulated a thousand times : *struggles are carried on by most dissimilar methods.* In short, economic, political, and intellectual competition will never cease among men. Hence antagonism will always exist, but as soon as men stop butchering one another solidarity among them will be established.

The co-existence of antagonism and solidarity may be observed in all human groups. Children in a class, for instance, vie with one another for the place at the head of the class, but they have a feeling of solidarity, and let a difference with another class arise, and they will act as a unit. Let the Chinese arm 36,000,000 soldiers[1] to-morrow to destroy Occidental

[1] The number of armed Europeans serving in regiments is about one to every 100 inhabitants. If China were as well organised from a military point of view, she could send this number of men to the field.

civilisation, and the Germans, French, English, Italians, and Russians, so widely separated to-day, would immediately form an alliance and make common cause.

Mr. Gumplowicz and the other apologists of bloodshed commit a further mistake. They are extremely short-sighted. They fancy that man's one enemy is man. That is not so. Man has other infinitely more dangerous and crueller enemies. These are climatic conditions and certain animal and vegetable species. How many millions of our fellow-men are carried off annually by the microbe of tuberculosis, not to mention the microbes of cholera and the bubonic plague! The phylloxera has cost France more than the five milliards of the Prussian indemnity. Innumerable parasites attack our crops and cause thousands of men to die of hunger and poverty. In addition, how

much suffering do not the cold of our
climate and the heat of the tropics cause?
Count up the many, many victims
of those two agents alone, not to speak
of storms, hail, floods, and droughts.
The unfortunates who die from those
scourges number millions.

A common enemy produces allies.
The Germans fought one another in
1866. Four years later they united
against the common enemy, the French.
Europe, so profoundly divided, would be
united against China. When we shall
cease to be blinder than moles, we shall
understand the elementary truth that the
questions dividing the civilised nations
are mere bagatelles, bits of folly and
puerility. To shed torrents of blood for
the possession of a province is an act of
childishness. Our awfullest enemies, the
elements and germs and insect destroyers,
attack us every minute without cease,

yet we murder one another as if we were
out of our senses. Death is ever on the
watch for us, and we think of nothing
but to snatch a few patches of land!
About 5,000,000,000 days of work go
every year to the displacement of boundary lines. Think of what humanity
could obtain if that prodigious effort were
devoted to fighting our real enemies, the
noxious species and our hostile environment. We should conquer them in a
few years. The entire globe would turn
into a model farm. Every plant would
grow for our use. The savage animals
would disappear, and the infinitely tiny
animals would be reduced to impotence
by hygiene and cleanliness. The earth
would be conducted according to our
convenience. In short, the day men
realise who their worst enemies are, they
will form an alliance against them, they
will cease to murder one another like

wild beasts from sheer folly. Then they will be the true rulers of the planet, the lords of creation.

Of old, man was the game hunted by man. In our modern States, immense communities of mutual spoliation, man is more frequently the slave of man. We shall attain the culmination of prosperity realisable here below when man becomes the ally of man.

THE END

R. CLAY AND SONS, LTD., BRUNSWICK ST., S.E., AND BUNGAY SUFFOLK.

THE GREAT ILLUSION

A Study of the Relation of Military Power in Nations to their Economic and Social Advantage

BY

NORMAN ANGELL

One Vol., Cr. 8vo, price 2s. 6d. net

LONDON : WILLIAM HEINEMANN

"THE GREAT ILLUSION" AND PUBLIC OPINION.

"The Daily Mail."

No book has attracted wider attention or has done more to stimulate thought in the present century than " The Great Illusion." Published obscurely, and the work of an unknown writer, it gradually forced its way to the front. . . . Has become a significant factor in the present discussion of armaments and arbitration.

"The Daily Chronicle."

Mr. Angell has compelled, on the part of all honest readers, a new mode of thinking on the whole question of war. . . . The most pregnant half-crown's worth in Europe to-day.

"Nation."

No piece of political thinking has in recent years more stirred the world which controls the movement of politics. . . . A fervour, a simplicity, and a force which no political writer of our generation has equalled . . . rank its author, with Cobden among the greatest of our pamphleteers, perhaps the greatest since Swift.

"Edinburgh Review."

Mr. Angell's main thesis cannot be disputed, and when the facts . . . are fully realised, there will be another diplomatic revolution more fundamental than that of 1756.

"Daily News."

So simple were the questions he asked, so unshakable the facts of his reply, so enormous and dangerous the popular illusion which he exposed, that the book not only caused a sensation in reading circles, but also, as we know, greatly moved certain persons high-placed in the political world.

The critics have failed to find a serious flaw in Norman Angell's logical, coherent, masterly analysis.

Mr. Henry W. Nevinson in Conway Memorial Lecture, March 17, 1911.

A book that will leave its mark not only on the mind, but, I think, on the actual and external history of man.

PUBLIC OPINION ON "THE GREAT ILLUSION"

Sir Harry Johnston in " Nineteenth Century and After," December, 1910.

Nothing that has ever been written has come so near proving successfully the futility of all great wars. . . . All persons of any nationality which has warlike tendencies should read this remarkable book.

Sir Frank Lascelles (formerly British Ambassador at Berlin) in Speech at Glasgow, January 29, 1912.

While I was staying with the late King his Majesty referred me to a book which had then been published by Norman Angell entitled " The Great Illusion." I read the book, and while I think that at present it is not a question of practical politics, I am convinced that it will change the thought of the world in the future.

Mr. Harold Begbie in the " Daily Chronicle."

A new idea is suddenly thrust upon the minds of men. . . . It is hardly an exaggeration to say that this book does more to fill the mind with the intolerable weight of war, to convince the reasonable mind . . . than all the moral and eloquent appeals of Tolstoy. . . . The wisest piece of writing on the side of peace extant in the world to-day.

" Birmingham Post."

" The Great Illusion," by sheer force, originality, and indisputable logic, has won its way steadily forward, and made its author a person to be quoted by statesmen and diplomatists, not only in England, but in France, Germany, and America.

"Glasgow News."

If only for the daring with which Mr. Angell's extraordinary book declares that the accepted ideas are so much moonshine, it would be a work to attract attention. When we add that Mr. Angell makes out a decidedly brilliant and arresting case for his contention, we have said sufficient to indicate that it is worth perusal by the most serious type of reader.

"The Western Mail."

A novel, bold and startling theory.

" Western Daily Press."

To many the ideas of the writer will seem at first to be absolutely revolutionary. . . . The train of thought is so unusual that Mr. Angell must not expect immediate agreement. . . . The book is a really valuable and original contribution to the study of the most alarming political problem of the present day.

COLONIAL OPINION.

Mr. W. M. Hughes, Acting Premier of Australia, in letter to the "Sydney Telegraph."

It is a great book, a glorious book to read. It is a book pregnant with the brightest promise to the future of civilised man. Peace—not the timid, shrinking figure of the Hague, cowering under the sinister shadow of six million bayonets—appears at length as an ideal possible of realisation in our own time.

PUBLIC OPINION ON "THE GREAT ILLUSION"

Sir George Reid, Australian High Commissioner in London (Sphinx Club Banquet, May 5, 1911).

I regard the author of this book as having rendered one of the greatest services ever rendered by the writer of a book to the human race. Well, I will be very cautious indeed—one of the greatest services which any author has rendered during the past hundred years.

"Sydney Bulletin."

No publication of recent years has had such an important effect in so short a time. . . . A very valuable book. By far the most notable contribution of recent years to the anti-war propaganda. It clears away many of the mists that have gathered round the subject.

"The Western Mail" (Perth).

Far and away the greatest exposure of the folly of modern armaments in the literature of the world.

"South African Weekly Standard."

Certainly the most masterly and telling argument in favour of peace that the world has yet seen.

AMERICA.

"New York Times," March 12, 1911.

A book which has compelled thought; a book full of real ideas deserves the welcome it has received. The author is enjoying the almost unlimited praise of his contemporaries, expressed or indicated by many men of eminence and influence, by countless reviewers who have lately hungered for a hero to worship.

Moreover . . . it certainly makes for genuine æsthetic pleasure, and that is all most of us ask of a book.

"The Evening Post," Chicago (Mr. Floyd Dell), February 17, 1911.

The book, being read, does not simply satisfy curiosity; it disturbs and amazes. It is not, as one would expect, a striking expression of some familiar objections to war. It is instead—it appears to be—a new contribution to thought, a revolutionary work of the first importance, a complete shattering of conventional ideas about international politics: something corresponding to the epoch-making "Origin of Species" in the realm of biology.

All of this it appears to be. One says "appears," not because the book fails completely to convince, but because it convinces so fully. The paradox is so perfect there must be something wrong about it! . . .

At first glance the statement which forms the basis of the book looks rather absurd; but before it is finished it seems a self-evident proposition. It is certainly a proposition which if proved will provide a materialistic common-sense basis for disarmament. . . .

There is subject matter here for ironic contemplation. Mr. Angell gives the reader no chance to imagine that these things "just happened." He shows why they happened and had to happen.

. . . . .

One returns again and again to the arguments, looking to find some fallacy in them. Not finding them, one stares wonderingly ahead into the future, where the book seems to cast its portentous shadow.

PUBLIC OPINION ON "THE GREAT ILLUSION"

"Boston Herald," January 21, 1911.

This is an epoch-making book, which should be in the hands of everyone who has even the slightest interest in human progress. . . . His criticism is not only masterly—it is overwhelming; for though controversy will arise on some of the details, the main argument is irrefutable. He has worked it out with a grasp of the evidence and a relentlessness of logic that will give life and meaning to his book for many a year to come.

"North American" (Philadelphia).

This unpretentious 400-page volume has done—and is probably doing—more important service in the interest of permanent peace than any other agency of appeal to pure reason in the minds of men.

"St. Louis Globe-Democrat."

Mr. Angell throws into the dust-bin the worn-out theories, the axioms of statecraft, the shibboleths of diplomats, the mouthings of politicastros as to the necessity for war. A brilliant arraignment . . . an altogether splendid monograph.

"Everybody's Magazine."

Mr. Angell has a mind like an edged blade, but he uses it like a scientist, and not like a crusader. He is not a propagandist, he is an elucidator. His book is not a plea, it is a demonstration.

"Life" (New York).

An inquiry into the nature and history of the forces that have shaped and are shaping our social development that throws more light upon the meaning and the probable outcome of the so-called "war upon war" than all that has been written and published upon both sides put together. The incontrovertible service that Mr. Angell has rendered us in "The Great Illusion" is to have introduced intellectual order into an emotional chaos.

FRANCE, BELGIUM, AND GERMANY.

"La Petite République" (M. Henri Turot), 17 Décembre, 1910.

J'estime, pour ma part, "Le Grande Illusion" doit avoir, au point de vue de la conception moderne de l'économie politique internationale, un retentissement égal à celui qu'eut, en matière biologique, la publication, par Darwin, de "l'Origine des espèces."

C'est que M. Norman Angell joint à l'originalité de la pensée le courage de toutes les franchises, qu'il unit à une prodigieuse érudition la lucidité d'esprit et la méthode qui font jaillir la loi scientifique de l'ensemble des événements observés.

"L'Eclair" (M. E, Judet), 30 Juin, 1911.

Le livre de Norman Angell a soulevé des enthousiasmes indescriptibles. Certes, il vaut la peine d'êter lu attentivement.

"Revue Bleu," Mai, 1911.

Fortement étayées, ses propositions émanent d'un esprit singulièrement réaliste, également informé et clairvoyant, qui met une connaissance des affaires et une dialectique concise au service d'une conviction, aussi passionnée que généreuse.

4

PUBLIC OPINION ON "THE GREAT ILLUSION"

"Le Rappel," 24 Février, 1911.

La thèse est soutenue d'une façon extraordinairement convainante et au moyen d'arguments que le plus subtil des économistes, des sociologues ou des historiens ne saurait réfuter.

"La Dépêche de Toulouse."

Le dangereux branle-bas auquel se prête en ce moment l'Europe rend la lecture des thèses que défend, avec une minutieuse audace M. Norman Angell, passionante plus que jamais.

Au surplus, dès aujourd'hui, qui oserait dire que des arguments analogues à ceux que fait valoir M. Norman Angell ne pèsent pas, et d'un poids très lourd dans la balance des gouvernements?

M. Jean Jaurès, during debate in French Chamber of Deputies, January 13, 1911 : see Journal Officiel, 14 Janvier, 1911.

Il a paru, il y a peu de temps, un livre anglais de M. Norman Angell, "La Grand Illusion," qui a produit un grand effet en Angleterre. Dans les quelques jours que j'ai passés de l'autre côté du détroit, j'ai vu, dans les réunions populaires, toutes les fois qu'il était fait mention de ce livre, les applaudissements éclater.

Extract from Speech in the French Senate of Le Rapporteur du Budget des Colonies, Journal Officiel, 2 Juillet, 1911.

A ce sujet, il convient de signaler la thèse si particulièrement intéressante de M. Norman Angell dans son œuvre la "Grand Illusion."

Il est évident qu'il y a là une vue des plus suggestives, et cela doit être pour nous un sujet de méditation, au moment même où nous voulons organiser et administrer nos nouvelles possessions. (*Très bien ! très bien !*)

"Le Peuple," Bruxelles. (M. Maurice Sluys), 4 Mai, 1911.

Par l'impression énorme qu'il a produite, les polémiques sans fin qu'il a suscitées dans les journaux du monde entier, M. Angell a fait un bien inestimable à la cause de la paix. . . .

C'est avec une vraie joie que j'ai lu le livre de M. Angell, que j'ai suivi son style clair et nerveux. Les polémiques en réponse aux critiques que sa thèse souleva sont de vrais modèles de journalisme compétent, honnête et verveux, vidant les formules et les lieux communs des militaristes, des politiciens, des diplomates et des sous-diplomates plus dangereux encore, qui encombrent les officines des journaux et déversent leur prose sensationnelle et malfaisante. Je n'ai pas en main la traduction française de la "Grand Illusion," je ne sais si elle a conservé toute la fraîcheur d'improvisation et de clarté de style de l'original, mais ce qu'elle n'a pu lui faire perdre, c'est la force de son argumentation, précise, évidente, irréfutable—et irréfutée jusqu'ici d'ailleurs.

Professor Karl von Bar, the authority on International and Criminal Law, Privy Councillor, etc.

Particularly do I agree with the author in these two points : (1) That in the present condition of organised society the attempt of one nation to destroy the commerce or industry of another must damage the victor more perhaps than the vanquished; and (2) that physical force is a constantly diminishing factor in human affairs. The rising generation seems to be realising this more and more.

Dr. Friedrich Curtius.

The book will, I hope, convince everyone that in our time the attempt to settle industrial and commercial conflicts by arms is an absurdity. . . . I doubt, indeed, whether educated folks in Germany entertain this "illusion" . . . or the idea that colonies or wealth can be "captured." . . . A war

5

PUBLIC OPINION ON "THE GREAT ILLUSION"

dictated by a moral ideal, the only one we can justify, is inconceivable as between England and Germany.

Professor Walthar Schuecking, writer on International Law.

Norman Angell has shown—and it is the first time such has been shown in this compelling way—the real economic and political foundations of the contemporary world, the foundations on which future peace will be inevitably built.

Dr. Wilhelm Ostwald, who has occupied chairs in several German Universities, as well as at Harvard and Columbia.

From the first line to the last "The Great Illusion" expresses my own opinions.

Dr. Sommer, Member of the Reichstag.

A most timely work, and one which everyone, be he statesman or political economist, should study.

Dr. Hans Wehberg, well-known political writer, author of "The Right of Capture," which has just appeared in English (King and Son).

Heartily welcome the book. . . . Have myself defended a similar point of view in my "Right of Capture." . . . Disagree on one point only: Mr. Angell does not seem sufficiently to appreciate the moral motives of progress.

Dr. Max Nordau.

If the destiny of people were settled by reason and interest, the influence of such a book would be decisive. . . . The book will convince the far-seeing minority, who will spread the truth, and thus slowly conquer the world.

Friedrich von Payer, Member of the Reichstag.

The book has made a great and favourable impression upon me.

Pastor Karl Jentsch, author of "The Future of the German Race."

I have myself often pointed out the difference in economic conditions in the 20th and the 16th or 17th century. . . . Conquest of one equally civilised nation by another is, as the author shows, sheer futility, but the German domination of (say) Asia Minor, its better organisation and development, would be for the benefit of the world. . . . It is to be hoped that the book will help to make plain that Germany's future expansion is not towards the West, where she desires to have sincere friends, but towards the less organised East.

Dr. Albert Suedekum, Member of the Reichstag, author of several works on municipal government, editor of Municipal Year-books, etc.

I consider the book an invaluable contribution to the better understanding of the real basis of international peace.

Dr. Otto Mugdan, Member of the Reichstag, Member of the National Loan Commission, Chairman of the Audit Commission, etc.

The demonstration of the financial interdependence of modern civilised nations, and the economic futility of conquest, could not be made more irrefutably.

Dr. Hugo Ganz, author and journalist.

By its complete and humorous refutation of some of the basic errors of politics, the book has proved a rare pleasure to me. It has *proved* what I have long vaguely *felt*, and I cherish the hope that its spread may work immeasurable good. . . . I endorse every line.

6

PUBLIC OPINION ON "THE GREAT ILLUSION"

A. C. Strahl (" K. Schrader "), Member of the Reichstag, author and playwright.

I have been particularly struck by the importance of the thesis embodied in "The Great Illusion," and thoroughly agree. I shall take an early opportunity of calling attention to it in the Reichstag.

FINANCIAL AND ECONOMIC AUTHORITIES.

"Economist" (London).

Nothing has ever been put in the same space so well calculated to set plain men thinking usefully on the subject of expenditure on armaments, scare and war. . . . The result of the publication of this book has been within the past month or two quite a number of rather unlikely conversions to the cause of retrenchment.

"Investor's Review," November 12, 1910.

No book we have read for years has so interested and delighted us. . . . He proceeds to argue, and to prove, that conquests do not enrich the conqueror under modern conditions of life, that there is no relation between military prowess and trade prosperity, unless it be the relation of the mistletoe to the oak, and that real wealth-bringing indemnities cannot be exacted. The days of loot worth gathering are over among civilised nations, whose wealth is so largely a matter of documents and book entries. . . . The style in which the book is written—sincere, transparent, simple, and now and then charged with fine touches of ironic humour—make it very easy to read.

"Journal of the Institute of Bankers of Great Britain."

One of the most brilliant contributions to the literature of international political relations which has appeared for a very long time. Whether or no the reader agrees with all the conclusions, he cannot but admire the cogency of the reasoning, and will be forced to admit that on many points the writer's arguments are irresistible. Those members who have not read it should lose no time in doing so.

"American Journal of Political Economy."

The best treatise yet written on the economic aspect of war.

"American Political Science Review."

It may be doubted whether within its entire range the peace literature of the Anglo-Saxon world has ever produced a more fascinating or significant study.

"Journal des Economistes."

Son livre sera beaucoup lu, car il est aussi agréable que profond, et il donnera beaucoup à réfléchir.

"La Bourse de Paris."

A quelques mois d'échéance, la crise financière et boursière, née de l'incident Frano-Allemand, démontre que M. Angell n'a pas toujours cheminé dans le domaine de l'utopie et que nombre de ses arguments méritent d'être retenus.

La leçon d'Agadir aura-t-elle été suffisamment cuisante . . . l'auteur de " La Grande Illusion " peut prétendre avec raison que nos idées en matière de politique intérieure ou extérieure sont toujours dominées par les errements d'antan, alors que le développement et la rapidité des communications ont complètement modifié les données et cette politique.

PUBLIC OPINION ON "THE GREAT ILLUSION"

"Export" (Organ des Central vereins für Handelsgeographie.)

By reason of its statement of the case against war in terms of practical politics and commercial advantage *Real-und Handelspolitikers*), the keenness and the mercilessness of the logic by which the author explodes the errors and the illusions of the war phantasists . . . the sense of reality, the force with which he settles accounts point by point with the militarists, this book stands alone. It is unique.

MILITARY OPINION,

"United Service Magazine," May, 1911.

It is an extraordinarily clearly written treatise upon an absorbingly interesting subject, and it is one which no thinking soldier should neglect to study. . . . As a rule, to the soldier or sailor, this type of literature is exasperating; because the problem set out to be proved and the opinions quoted in proving it run counter to his knowledge and experience. His vanity also is apt to be wounded, because the peace advocate often affects to regard the military profession as one confined to numskulled and chauvinistic individuals and usually ignores the results of the soldier's knowledge and experience, under the delusion that the latter's patriotism as a citizen is certain to be tainted where his own bread and butter is in question. . . . Mr. Angell's book is much to be commended in this respect. It contains none of the nauseating sentiment which is normally parasitic to "peace" literature. The author is evidently careful to take things exactly as he conceives them to be, and to work out his conclusions without "cleverness," and unobscured by technical language. His method is to state the case for the defence (of present-day "militarist" statecraft), to the best of his ability in one chapter, calling the best witnesses he can find and putting their views from every standpoint so clearly that even one who was beforehand quite ignorant of the subject cannot fail to understand. Mr. Angell's book is one which all citizens would do well to read, and read right through. It has the clearness of vision and the sparkling conciseness which one associates with Swift at his best.

"The Army Service Corps Quarterly," April, 1911.

The ideas are so original and clever, and in places are argued with so much force and common-sense, that they cannot be pushed aside at once as preposterous. . . . There is food here for profound study. . . . Above all, we should encourage the sale of "The Great Illusion" abroad, among nations likely to attack us, as much as possible.

"War Office Times."

Should be read by everyone who desires to comprehend both the strength and the weakness of this country.

"Army and Navy Journal" (N.Y.), October 5, 1910.

If all anti-militarists could argue for their cause with the candour and fairness of Norman Angell we should welcome them, not with "bloody hands to hospitable graves," but to a warm and cheery intellectual comradeship. Mr. Angell has packed away in his book more common-sense than peace societies have given birth to in all the years of their existence. . . . We have nowhere, in all the literature on peace and war that we have read, found a clearer presentation of the sentiment behind military preparations than that given by Mr. Angell in his first chapter . . . is worth a whole library of the sentimental fustian which has been too long masquerading as representing the highest aspirations of mankind for universal peace.

A LIST OF
CURRENT FICTION

PUBLISHED BY

WILLIAM HEINEMANN
AT 21 BEDFORD ST., LONDON, W.C.

HE WHO PASSED
To M. L. G. (Anon.) 6/-

" As a story, it is one of the most enthralling I have read
for a long time . . . Six—seven o'clock struck—half-
past-seven—and yet this extraordinary narrative of a
woman's life held me absolutely enthralled . . . I forgot
the weather ; I forgot my own grievances ; I forgot everything, in fact, under the spell of this wonderful book.
. . . . In fact the whole book bears the stamp of reality
from cover to cover. There is hardly a false or strained
note in it. It is the ruthless study of a woman's life. . .
If it is not the novel of the season, the season is not likely
to give us anything much better."—*The Tatler.*

THE SECRET GARDEN
by Mrs. HODGSON BURNETT 6/-

Author of " The Shuttle," " Little Lord Fauntleroy," etc.
Large Cr. 8vo, with coloured Illustrations by CHARLES ROBINSON.

" The treatment by the authoress is as skilled in technique
and vivid in human interest as the reader would expect
from her. . . The illustrations by Mr. Charles Robinson
are the work of an artist rarely gifted."—*Daily Telegraph.*

LITTLE BROTHER
by GILBERT CANNAN 6/-
Author of "Devious Ways," "Peter Homunculus."

" Mr. Gilbert Cannan's new novel is an intensely interesting study of an unusual personality—brimming over with
ideas, with humour, satire and observation, and good to
read . . . . fascinating even when most provocative. . .
' Little Brother ' is far and away the best and most
interesting novel that the year has so far yielded."—*Globe.*

LOVE'S PILGRIMAGE
by UPTON SINCLAIR 6/-
Author of "The Jungle," "King Midas," etc.

" Mr. Upton Sinclair has written around such a great subject with such marvellous intuition and skill, and has presented so many problems which are engaging general attention, that all feminists and theorists upon social subjects will be eager to read his latest book."

—*Daily Telegraph.*

PASSION FRUIT
by E. C. VIVIAN 6/-

" The interest all through depends mainly upon the male characters, who are drawn with unusual vigour and certainty. . . . The book as a whole is marked by a breadth of handling which sets it apart from the average novel."—*Morning Post.*

" ' Passion Fruit ' is the work of a past-master in story telling."—*Sheffield Independent.*

BORROWERS OF FORTUNE
by JESSIE LECKIE HERBERTSON 6/-
Author of "Young Life," etc.

A novel of happier vein than has sometimes been the case with Miss Herbertson. Her lighter heart is as infectious as her gravity was impressive.

MAJORIE STEVENS
by V. TAUBMAN-GOLDIE 6/-
Author of " Nigel Thomson."

" Presented . . . with some literary power and insight into the springs of human action . . . with tact, good taste, and a whole-hearted desire to get at the truth. We hope to meet the author again—and soon."

—*Pall Mall Gazette.*

21 BEDFORD STREET, LONDON, W.C.

JOHN CHRISTOPHER:

I. Dawn and Morning.　II. Storm and Stress.

by ROMAIN ROLLAND　　　　each 6/-

Translated by GILBERT CANNAN. Author of "Little Brother," etc.

> "To most readers he will be a revelation, a new interest in their lives. Take the book up where you will, and you feel interested at once. You can read it and re-read it. It never wearies nor grows irritating."
> —*The Daily Telegraph.*

> "His English exercises so easy an effect that the reader has never for an instant the irritating sense of missing beauties through the inadequacies of a borrowed language; we have also compared it in many cases with the original and found it remarkably accurate. Readers may then be assured that they will lose but little of Mr. Rolland's beauty and wisdom, even though they are unable to read him in the original, and Mr. Cannan is to be warmly congratulated."—*The Standard.*

JOHN CHRISTOPHER IN PARIS

by ROMAIN ROLLAND　　　　6/-

Translated by GILBERT CANNAN. Author of "Peter Homunculus," etc.

> "A noble piece of work, which must, without any doubt whatever, ultimately receive the praise and attention which it so undoubtedly merits. . . There is hardly a single book more illustrative, more informing and more inspiring, . . . than M. Romain Rolland's creative work, 'John Christopher'."—Extract from descriptive review in *The Daily Telegraph.*

Ready Shortly :

JOHN CHRISTOPHER : The End of the Journey

Translated by GILBERT CANNAN, Author of "Devious Ways."

---

21 BEDFORD STREET, LONDON, W.C.

A PORTENTOUS HISTORY
by ALFRED TENNYSON   6/-

" With considerable skill we are shown how ignorant and conventional prejudice of all the normal inhabitants of the village are roused against the poor, good giant, only because he is greater than they are. Mr. Tennyson gives a vivid and unpleasant picture of prejudice and instinctive cruelty. In Mr. Tennyson we have a new novelist with something real and weighty to say."—*Westminster Gazette.*

THE MAGIC OF THE HILL
by DUNCAN SCHWANN   6/-
Author of "The Book of a Bachelor," etc.

" The book is in fact, to be read for its light-hearted pictures of modern Paris, Paris seen with eyes of someone who knows it intimately and loves it. Mr. Schwann has more than a little of Thackeray's absorbing interest in minor characters, minor events, and minor problems. The book proves that Mr. Schwann, as a student of life, has the right touch and the right humour."—*The Standard.*

HER HUSBAND'S COUNTRY
by SYBIL SPOTTISWOODE   6/-
Author of "Marcia in Germany," etc.

" Despite its tragic core, the story is delightfully fresh and amusing, and presents on the whole an attractive picture of German life. The 'Hausfrau' in particular is treated with much appreciation and sympathy."—*The Athenæum.*

" Delightful as were her earlier books, her new novel shows a great advance, for here she gets down to the heart of things, to the bed-rock of human nature. In Patience she develops a character with real power and insight." —*Westminster Gazette.*

21 BEDFORD STREET, LONDON, W.C.

ZULEIKA DOBSON
by MAX BEERBOHM   6/-

"In a word, he has achieved a masterpiece. He has
written a book in which wit and invention never flag:
a book, the writing of which he has enjoyed so tremen-
dously that the reader enjoys it with him, as it were,
personally, a book that is all of a piece, never halts, never
drops; a book that is a sheer delight from cover to cover."
—Alfred Sutton in *The Daily Mail.*

THE DEVOURERS
by ANNIE VIVANTI CHARTRES   6/-

"The book is delightfully written. . . . Mrs. Chartres
has humour, she has style, she has pathos."—*The Standard.*

"It is a great feat for any author to succeed in interesting
her readers in three successive generations of heroines
within the covers of a single novel without diminution of
sympathy; yet that feat has been accomplished in 'The
Devourers' . . . it is an irresistible story and full of
sympathetic charm."—*The Evening Standard.*

THE HOUSE OF BONDAGE
by C. G. COMPTON   6/-
Author of "Her Own Devices," etc.

"It says something for Mr. Compton's power of writing,
that, while Laura transgresses the ordinary code, not by
misfortune but by free will, she still remains ordinarily
sympathetic. The plot of the story is well worked out,
and some of the minor characters are excellent."—
Truth.

"His easy, graceful writing is very pleasant to read."
—*The English Review.*

A LIKELY STORY
by WILLIAM DE MORGAN   6/-

"How delightful it all is. . . Mr. De Morgan is worth having for himself alone and for the point of view of the world that he shows us."—*Standard.*

"The book is great fun. . . Much amusement, much cause for sly chuckling throughout the book. . . I have enjoyed every line of it."—*T.P.'s Weekly.*

"You cannot resist the charm of the narrator, who makes you feel as if you were listening to an improvisation."—*The Spectator.*

Author of

JOSEPH VANCE	IT NEVER CAN HAPPEN
ALICE FOR SHORT	AGAIN
AN AFFAIR OF DISHONOUR	SOMEHOW GOOD

SIR GUY AND LADY RANNARD
by H. N. DICKINSON   6/-
Author of "Keddy," etc.

"Extraodinarily clever indeed is this study. Apart from the absorbing interest of the two central characters, the book is full of able and suggestive studies. The whole book is one of the most remarkable that a young man has produced for many a long year."—*Morning Post.*

THE MAGNATE
by ROBERT ELSON   6/-

"It is a story that every reader will recommend after reading it—and with excellent reason, for it is fresh, original, and powerfully written."—*Daily Graphic.*

"Mr. Elson has what Dickens and Thackeray and other great writers of fiction have. He has a personality. 'The Magnate' is quite the freshest story that we have read for a long time. We have no hesitation in recommending it to all persons who like a novel which is full of thought and detail and brims over with optimism."—*Daily Mail.*

21 BEDFORD STREET, LONDON, W.C.

THE WHITE PROPHET
by HALL CAINE 6/-

"These volumes are in every way a pleasure to read. Of living authors, Mr. Hall Caine must certainly sway as multitudinous a following as any living man. A novel from his pen has become indeed for England and America something of an international event."—*Times.*

"Whether regarded as a romance or as a contribution to political history, it is an ample and interesting perform-ance."—*The Daily Graphic.*

Author of

THE BONDMAN	THE ETERNAL CITY
CAPT'N DAVEY'S HONEY-MOON	THE MANXMAN
THE LAST CONFESSION	THE PRODIGAL SON
THE BLIND MOTHER	THE SCAPEGOAT
THE CHRISTIAN	

MRS. DRUMMOND'S VOCATION
by MARK RYCE 6/-

"There is no doubt that 'Mrs. Drummond's Vocation' is a book full of vitality and freshness. Each scene is perfectly natural and clear cut, and the characters are wonderfully close to life. Writing so engagingly simple, so economical a use of words, and so picturesque a gift of description."
—*The Morning Leader.*

THE MARRIAGE OF CAPTAIN KETTLE
by C. CUTCLIFFE HYNE 6/-
Author of "Captain Kettle," etc.

Once more we have our little firebrand, as plucky, as hard hitting, and as nigger-driving as ever, as sentimental and as lovable. This time, as is told in the title, Fate offers compensation for the many knocks she has dealt him.

THE PILGRIM KAMANITA
by CARL GJELLERUP   6/-

"Behind the imagination which floats 'The Pilgrim Kamanita' above the common there is a solid background of historical study which enables Mr. Gjellerup to make his characters and his scenes real. He has managed to catch the atmosphere of ancient India, and so wrap it about every place and act and speech in the story that the illusion and spell are on us from beginning to end. . . . It is a real romance, full of life and colour—and such colour as only India, in the full sensuous splendour of Hindu rites, can offer. . . It is a beautiful allegory of the higher life, full of suggestion and even inspiration for those who have ears to hear. Mr. Gjellerup is to be congratulated not only on a noble idea, most skilfully presented, but also upon a translator who hardly ever lets us feel that we are not reading the original."—*Times.*

THE PATRICIAN
by JOHN GALSWORTHY   6/-

"I cannot find better praise than which to sum up Mr. Galsworthy's ' Patrician' than the one that it is 'deeply interesting'. Indeed, there is a vividness about the whole story which is absolutely fascinating. It lingers in the memory long, long after other novels of a less distinguished but more thrilling nature have been completely forgotten.
—*The Tatler.*

Author of

THE COUNTRY HOUSE	THE ISLAND PHARISEES
FRATERNITY	THE MAN OF PROPERTY
A MOTLEY	

THE GUEST OF QUESNAY
by BOOTH TARKINGTON   6/-

"Mr. Booth Tarkington's spirit and freshness carry him successfully through ' The Guest of Quesnay'. He is an admirable story-teller. Mr. Tarkington's story goes briskly, and its human beings are sketched with skill and ease; it is therefore altogether readable."—*Athenæum.*

21 BEDFORD STREET, LONDON, W.C.

TALES OF THE UNEASY
by VIOLET HUNT   6/-
Author of "The Wife of Altamont," "The Sheep Stealers," etc.

"Miss Violet Hunt is eminently skilful, albeit a relentless 'raconteuse', the light of her inspiration burns with a hard gemlike flame. Miss Hunt has gained greatly in craftmanship during the last few years : her style is excellent, her grip of subjects sure, and her insight exceptionally clear and sane."—*The Athenæum.*

ESTHER
by AGNES E. JACOMB   6/-

"The book is well written and the characters are well drawn."—*Pall Mall Gazette.*

"Miss Jacomb has written in 'Esther' a very interesting novel ; its situations are original, and the characters are sufficiently individual to make a convincing whole. . . ."
—*Morning Post.*

THE GETTING OF WISDOM
by HENRY HANDEL RICHARDSON   6/-
Author of "Maurice Guest."

"An extraordinarily intimate and sympathetic study of a little girl and of the influence school-life has upon her gives unusual charm and interest to this story."
—*Daily Mail.*

"'Stalky for Girls' might very well be the sub-title of Mr. Richardson's story. What 'Stalky & Co.' did for the boy, 'The Getting of Wisdom' tries to do for the girl. It is a bright, vivid piece of character writing."
—*Saturday Review.*

21 BEDFORD STREET, LONDON, W.C.

THE WHITE PEACOCK
by D. H. LAWRENCE   6/-

"A book of real distinction, both of style and thought. Many of the descriptive passages have an almost lyrical charm, and the characterisation is, generally speaking, deft and life-like. 'The White Peacock' is a book not only worth reading but worth reckoning with, for we are inclined to think that its author has come to stay."

—*Morning Post,*

LOVE LIKE THE SEA
by J. E. PATTERSON   6/-
Author of "Tillers of the Soil," etc.

"He tells his story to the sound of wind and waves, and if now and again his ardour for and knowledge of the sea leads him aside from the purpose of his scheme, the digressions are so admirably done that the book would lose from the point of view of literary interest were they omitted. . . . The three principal characters are well drawn (there are minor ones also excellently delineated)."

—*The Globe.*

BURNING DAYLIGHT
by JACK LONDON   6/-
Author of " The Call of the Wild," "Martin Eden," etc.

" I have long regarded the stories of Mr. Jack London as a welcome relief from the dulness of most contemporary fiction, and his latest, 'Burning Daylight,' did not disappoint me in this respect. No one who has read the author's previous works will need to be told with what wonderful skill the atmosphere of this grim and unfriendly land is conveyed. There is one chapter, especially, which tells how, for a bet, Daylight raced two thousand miles over an unbroken trail of ice in sixty days that seems to me absolutely the best piece of descriptive writing of its kind that ever I read."—*Punch.*

ADNAM'S ORCHARD
by SARAH GRAND 6/-

Author of

THE HEAVENLY TWINS	THE BETH BOOK
IDEALA	OUR MANIFOLD NATURE

etc., etc.

Mrs. Grand's new novel is notable for its powerful *motif*, and she touches in it upon one of the most burning problems of our day, namely :—the attitude of the great territorial families towards the people on the land. Quite apart from its undoubted qualities as a romance 'Adnam's Orchard' is a book of very immediate interest.

THE REWARD OF VIRTUE
by AMBER REEVES. 6/-

"There is cleverness enough and to spare, but it is . . . a spontaneous cleverness, innate, not laboriously acquired. . . . The dialogue . . . is so natural, so unaffected, that it is quite possible to read it without noticing the high artistic quality of it. . . . For a first novel Miss Reeves's is a remarkable achievement ; it would be a distinct achievement even were it not a first novel."

—Daily Chronicle.

THE COST OF IT
by ELEANOR MORDAUNT 6/-

Author of "The Garden of Contentment."

"Packed full of character and real life. . . . The character of the heroine is admirably drawn upon quite unconventional lines . . . . the situation is worked out with remarkable vigour and intensity. This is a fine, powerful and impressive novel, triumphing over inadequacies of literary training by sheer force of sincerity and of glowing human sentiment."*—Daily Telegraph.*

21 BEDFORD STREET, LONDON, W.C.

A PRINCE OF DREAMERS
by FLORA ANNIE STEEL

"This fascinating romance. The character of Akbar is drawn with sympathy and imaginative power; and the minor figures are equally convincing. Mrs. Steel knows how to reproduce in a way that few living writers can rival, the gorgeous colours, the subtle intrigues, the burning passions, and above all, the dreamy philosophy and poetic atmosphere of the East. It has many thrilling episodes told with admirable directness and force."

Author of —*Athenæum.*

THE FLOWER OF FORGIVE-
NESS
FROM THE FIVE RIVERS
THE HOSTS OF THE LORD
IN THE GUARDIANSHIP OF
GOD
IN THE PERMANENT WAY,
AND OTHER STORIES

MISS STUART'S LEGACY
ON THE FACE OF
THE WATERS
THE POTTER'S THUMB
RED ROWANS
A SOVEREIGN REMEDY
VOICES IN THE NIGHT

ESSENCE OF HONEYMOON
by H. PERRY ROBINSON 6/-

"Mr. Perry Robinson has never written a more fascinating and delightful little story than 'Essence of Honeymoon'. . . . Mr. Perry Robinson says exactly the right thing. . . . An inimitable piece of sporting fun, admirably carried out, and we can recommend no better literature for all young people about to be married, or even after they have taken that sobering step, than Mr. Perry Robinson's delightful pages."—*The Field.*

A PRISON WITHOUT A WALL
by RALPH STRAUS 6/-
Author of "The Scandalous Mr. Waldo."

"This beautiful, whimsical, tragic biography. We are lost in admiration of Mr. Straus' skill to portray the quintessential don. His pictures of combination room etiquette are literally to the life. But he knows also a wider world, and his touch is sure in drawing the eccentric great lady, the old-school politician, the passionate mondaine, and the fashionable charlatan. . . This perfectly told story."
—*Daily Mail.*

21 BEDFORD STREET, LONDON, W.C.

THE NOVELS OF LEO TOLSTOY
Translated by CONSTANCE GARNETT.

ANNA KARENIN 2/6 net

WAR AND PEACE 3/6 net

"Mrs. Garnett's translations from the Russian are always distinguished by most careful accuracy and a fine literary flavour. In this new rendering of Tolstoy she has surpassed herself."—*The Bookman.*

"Mrs. Garnett's translation has all the ease and vigour which Matthew Arnold found in French versions of Russian novels and missed in English. She is indeed so successful that, but for the names, one might easily forget he was reading a foreign author."
—*The Contemporary Review.*

THE NOVELS OF DOSTOEVSKY

"By the genius of Dostoevsky you are always in the presence of living, passionate characters. They are not puppets, they are not acting to keep the plot in motion. They are men and women—I should say you can hear them breathe—irresistibly moving to their appointed ends."—*Evening News.*

I. THE BROTHERS KARAMAZOV
3/6 net

Ready Shortly :

CRIME AND PUNISHMENT
Now for the first time translated in full from the Russian by CONSTANCE GARNETT, translator of the Novels of TURGENEV and TOLSTOY.

21 BEDFORD STREET, LONDON, W.C.